Be
True
to
Yourself

Be True to Yourself

A Daily Guide FOR Teenage GiRLS

Amanda Ford

Foreword by Shannon Berning

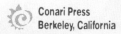

Conari Press
Berkeley, California

Conari Press books are distributed by Publishers Group West.
Cover Illustration/Photography: © Carol Kohen/ImageBank
Cover and book design: Claudia Smelser

ISBN: 1-57324-189-X

Library of Congress Cataloging-in-Publication Data

Ford, Amanda.
        Be true to yourself : daily meditations for teenage girls /
        Amanda Ford.
            p.   cm.
        Includes bibliographical references and index.
        ISBN 1–57324–189–X (trade paper : alk. paper)
        1. Teenage girls–Conduct of life. [1. Conduct of life. 2.
Youths' writings.] I. Title.
        BJ1651 .F67 2000
        158.1'28'08352—dc21

                                                    00-035886

Printed in Canada on recycled paper.
00 01 02 TC 10 9 8 7 6 5 4 3 2 1

To my listening ear, my encouragement,
my favorite friend, my inspiration—

my mom

Be True to Yourself

Foreword
by Shannon Berning, *Teen Voices* magazine

In sisterhood . . .

The closer we get to adulthood, the bigger everything gets. Our bodies curve outward and upward, our worlds expand further and further beyond our homes, and our knowledge grows more and more into the arena we once thought was reserved for adults. It's hard to keep up with all of our feelings and ideas. They're multiplying by the second. Unfortunately, the pressures in our lives seem to multiply, too!

Our families, friends, teachers, romantic interests, and the media all have messages for us—they want to tell us how to look, how to act, and what to want from our lives. What *we* want isn't always easy to figure out. With all this pressure, how do we get to the other side of our teen years in one piece? We need all the help we can get!

As Managing Editor of *Teen Voices*, a national magazine written by and for teen women, I know how much the stories of other young women can help us to become stronger ourselves. In *Be True to Yourself*, Amanda Ford offers to be our big sister for a year. At twenty years old, she recently made it into adulthood, and she's willing to share what she's learned from her experiences.

Amanda reminds us to accept compliments (because we deserve them), to love ourselves (because we need it), to support other young women (because it brings us up, too), and to write in our journals (because what we have to say is important)—and that's just the beginning! Amanda encourages us to use this book to take a break each day. We all have a million things to do, but we have to spend some time thinking about what we want from our lives and relationships.

As your world gets larger and larger, take what you can from *Be True to Yourself*. And keep thinking, dreaming, and growing—bigger and bigger!

The Sisters I Never Had

I never had a sister, but I always wished for two: an older *and* a younger sister. The older sister could enlighten me in the ways of the teen world. She would introduce me to older guys, give me fashion advice, tell me all the "how-to's" of kissing, and help me put on makeup for my big dates. I would flop onto her bed to cry about the boy who broke my heart, the friends who betrayed me, and my feelings of depression as she sat near, listening and comforting me. She would be there to lift my spirits when I didn't make the varsity volleyball team, when I failed my biology test, and when the hairdresser cut my hair so short that I looked like a boy.

With my younger sister, I could take over the role of guide. I would listen to her with an empathetic ear and remember what I felt like when I was in her place. I would teach her how to sneak out of the house without getting caught, let her study for her geometry final using my old test, and lend her my favorite outfit to wear on a night out with her friends. I would tell her about how I got a huge zit on the end of my nose the night before my first real date, and let her know she isn't the only girl who wishes she had a boyfriend. When she was sad, I would assure her that life always has a way of working out, and that soon things would get better. I would share my stories and give her advice so that she might get through the difficult teen years a little easier than I did.

Be True to Yourself has become the sisters I never had. It provides the encouragement and guidance I wished, as a teenager, that an older sister had given me, as well as stories and advice that I would share with my younger sister during her tumultuous teen years.

Be True to Yourself is set up as a book of daily thoughts and advice, but you don't have to use it like one. If the topic for a particular date doesn't fit you that day, look at the index in the back of the book, turn to a topic that interests you more, and go to that entry. Read this book every day, or read it randomly whenever you feel you need a little bit of guidance or support. Each entry is short and quick to read, but certain to help enhance your life.

Because I am only twenty years old, the teenager inside me is still vividly alive in my heart and mind. I can still feel the intense pain, joy, struggles, confusion, victories, and disappointments I encountered as a teen. Because I am twenty, I also have the ability to look back on my teenage years with a fresh perspective to see what mistakes I made and what things I did right. *Be True to Yourself* is everything I learned while being a teenage girl, and I hope it helps you like a big sister would as you grow from a little girl made of sugar and spice into the magnificent young woman you are becoming.

In January...

Clean and rearrange your bedroom to get the new year off to a fresh start.

Keep warm with a scarf of your favorite color and a mug of apple cider.

Buy a beautiful calendar for your room. Choose one with paintings, photography, inspirational quotes, flowers, or your favorite animals. Pick out something that reflects your personality and hang it where you can see it every day.

Life Is a Journey

Life is a journey, an eternal quest. You are searching for the ultimate treasure—yourself. You traveled down a paved, well-lit path as a child, but now that you are a teen, the journey has become more complicated. Who are you? What is the meaning of your life? What makes you happy? Things that seemed so clear at one time are now hazy and confusing.

Today is the beginning of a new year and it deserves a clean start. Be open to and excited about the experiences, challenges, and learning that await you this year. Remember that life is a journey; don't be discouraged if you aren't the smartest, prettiest, funniest, or most popular or athletic. The longer you travel through your teen years, the more you will learn about yourself and grow into the person *you* are meant to be.

Perfect Is Boring

One of my mom's CDs includes a duet with Art Garfunkel and his son James. The young boy doesn't sing on key or hit all the right notes, and it's obvious that he hasn't had any training in music, but that doesn't keep him from singing his heart out. The song is far from "perfect," but it definitely has character. It makes you smile, not to mention want to dance and sing along. Whenever my mom plays the song, I have young James Garfunkel's perky voice in my head for the rest of the day.

Why are we always getting down on ourselves for not being perfect? We always want to get straight A's, look like a model, or have everyone like us, but who wants to be perfect? Perfection is not possible; we all have flaws. Besides, it's boring! There is nothing interesting about perfection, and being flawless does not equal being the best. Today, remember that being comfortable with your imperfections is much better than being perfect.

Love Yourself

Did you know that there is something that can heal your hurt feelings, end your sense of self-consciousness, and give you a great deal of happiness? It exists, it's free, and it's available to everyone—it's self-love.

Self-love is not about being conceited and egotistical. It doesn't mean bragging, or putting someone else down to lift yourself up. Self-love is about accepting yourself as you are. It's loving your mind even if you don't always get A's, and loving your body even if it isn't the shape you want. It's allowing yourself to make mistakes instead of getting down on yourself for not being perfect.

Start loving yourself today. Instead of thinking, "I'll love myself when I lose five pounds," or, "I would be a better person if I had a boyfriend," try thinking, "I love myself the way I am, imperfections and all!" Be gentle with yourself, and know that you are lovable.

Receive Compliments

You are in art class when someone compliments the ceramic bowl you just made, and you say, "I think it's terrible. I totally messed it up." Later that day a friend says, "You look cute today!" and you respond, "No way! I hate my hair."

We girls often have a hard time accepting it when other people think we're good at things. When people give us compliments, we tend to dispute them with comments like, "That's not true," or, "Rachel's much better at that than I am." Statements like these don't allow us to accept the praise we get from others, and we maintain our negative self-images because we don't allow ourselves to take in the good stuff.

Today, accept all the compliments you are given. Instead of arguing or being modest, look the person in the eye, and say a sincere, "Thank you." Take in the compliment you are given, and keep those encouraging words with you throughout the day.

Keep a Journal

Today, get yourself a journal if you don't already have one. Buy a leather-bound journal, or one with flowers painted on the front. You can even make your own journal: use stationery and tie it with ribbons, or buy a spiral notebook and decorate the cover with a collage of magazine cut-outs. Your journal should be a book that reflects your personality, one that you will enjoy writing in.

Write in your journal as often as you'd like; write every day, or just when you need to vent your feelings. Describe what you did that day, how you are feeling, or what you hope will happen tomorrow. Don't censor anything; write whatever comes into your head. You will discover that keeping a journal helps you discover dreams that lie deep within your heart, put difficult feelings into words, and solve problems that have been troubling you. A journal is a girl's closest friend.

The I'm-Not-Good-Enough Buster

Have you ever convinced yourself that you aren't good enough? Sometimes when I go out with a group of my friends, I tell myself, "They don't really care if I'm here or not. Nobody thinks I'm funny or listens to me. They would have just as much fun if I wasn't here." Instead of joining the conversation, I just sit quietly, feeling insecure and convinced that nobody wants to hear what I have to say.

Today, before you go anywhere—into a classroom, the cafeteria, or sports practice—tell yourself, "Everyone in the room is going to be happy to see me. Their day will be better because I'm here!" This I'm-Not-Good-Enough Buster will help you overcome your fear of being rejected by people, and will bring out your most energetic self.

No More "I'm Not Mad At You"

Sometimes when I get mad, I give people the cold shoulder. I become quiet and say things like, "Nothing's wrong," or, "I'm not mad at you," even though I am obviously fuming inside. When I do this, I keep my anger bottled up inside instead of getting my feelings out in the open.

Using the cold shoulder tactic when you are mad at somebody will get you nowhere. If you are upset that your sister didn't come to your volleyball game like she promised, or hurt that your boyfriend didn't call when he said he would, let them know. Giving the cold shoulder will keep the other person in the dark about why you are mad at them, and doesn't help you resolve your angry feelings.

Today, tell somebody that you are mad at them and get your angry feelings out in the open. Work together to resolve them.

Beyond Sugar and Spice

"Sugar and spice and everything nice; that's what little girls are made of." I used to recite that rhyme, and as a child, it fit me. I was sweet, I never argued with my mom, and I smiled, played, and laughed innocently. Growing up meant that my sugar and spice got bumped aside by determination, passion, emotion, motivation, and desire. I developed a voice and a will of my own. I was no longer a little girl full of sugar and spice, but a teenager made of fire and ice and everything in between.

How wonderful to leave behind girlhood and become your own individual self! Next time that an adult argues that you are being "difficult," remind them that you are a complex person and have grown beyond simply sugar and spice. You are full of infinite variety! Today, let the world know that here comes an intelligent, fun-loving, strong-willed girl!

What's Important to You?

Values get hard to define when you are growing up and learning new things about life. It's hard to keep a set of values when your life and your opinions are constantly changing. Defining your values is important, though, because values are life's guidelines. They help you achieve the things that are important to you, and they are a way of showing that you respect yourself.

Today, take a few moments to define your values. In your journal, make a list of things that are important to you—friendships, getting good grades, honesty, getting along with your family, helping others, avoiding drugs and alcohol. Once you have your list, elaborate on the separate items. For example, under friendship you might write, "I value friends who listen when I'm sad, include me, and care about me. I value friends who are honest, hardworking, and fun to be with, and I want to be that type of friend for others."

Make Your Words Reality

It's not always easy to act on our values. I have often said, "I want to be less of a gossip," or, "I'm going to try to get straight A's," but sometimes I have trouble biting my tongue when I hear a rumor, or I talk on the phone when I should be studying for a history test.

Today, pick one of your value statements from yesterday and live it. Pay attention to your actions and make a conscious effort to hold that value. If you say that you value honesty, stop yourself when you are going to tell a white lie, and don't allow people to lie to you. Focus on a different value every day until you have made your values a natural part of your life.

Appreciate Yourself

What are you good at? What are your strengths? What are your best qualities? I bet these are hard questions to answer. However, if I asked you what you are bad at, what your weaknesses are, or what your worst qualities are, I bet you could answer without much thought. It's time to reverse your thinking and start focusing on your wonderful attributes.

Today, write down five positive things about yourself. Maybe you got a good grade on your Spanish test, or you cheered up someone who was feeling down. Write about how honest, friendly, hardworking, beautiful, and fun you are. Don't be afraid to brag about yourself; nobody will hear. There are many more wonderful things about yourself than there are bad; it's just that the good things are harder for you to see. Start appreciating yourself for the amazingly talented girl you are.

Take Good Care of Yourself

Think about your favorite possession. Maybe it's a teddy bear, a sweater, a photo album, or the telephone. Think about how well you care for that possession—you keep it clean, you are picky about whom you let touch it, and you would never lose it.

Now think about yourself—your body, your spirit, your mind. You are much more valuable than your favorite possession; you are absolutely irreplaceable. So why do you sometimes take better care of your belongings than you take care of yourself?

Today, treat yourself as your favorite thing. Take care of your body by eating healthy food and getting enough sleep. Nurture your spirit by spending time with people you care about and doing things you love. Engage your mind by reading good books and finishing your homework on time. You are valuable and worth being taken care of, so treat yourself well.

If He Says I'm Ugly, I Must Be Ugly

As soon as I turned the corner, I saw him—Andy Johnson, the love of my life! He looked so hot with his navy blue cap turned around backward, talking to his friend. As I walked past, I heard his friend say, "Dude, she's ugly."

"No kidding," Andy laughed.

It is devastating to hear people say bad things about you. It hurts your feelings and can ruin your self-esteem. It's easy to believe that if one person thinks you are ugly, then everyone must think you're ugly.

As hard as it is to do, you must not let negative comments get you down. Push them out of your mind; write them off as ignorant statements coming from an ignorant person. People will say bad things about you for many different reasons. Maybe they are jealous of you, or are just trying to be jerks. Today, remember that there are people who think you are pretty, smart, fun, and caring—you should think so too!

Do What You Want to Do

What do you do when you want to ask Jake to the upcoming Sadie Hawkins dance, but your best friend wants you to ask Garret because he's her date's best friend? What if your friend wants you to switch out of the painting class you love and into her computer class so that she won't be completely alone? There are many times when your friends will be pulling one way, but your heart will be pulling another.

Today, do what *you* want to do. By taking care of yourself, you are not being selfish. Selfishness is when you hurt others to get your way—when you lie, cheat, or don't care how your actions will affect someone else. Taking care of yourself means doing what's right for your well-being. It means making a decision based on what you know is best for you even when others want something else. You shouldn't rearrange your life or put your desires on hold to please other people.

Create Night Rituals

Glancing at the clock across the room, I said, "I've got to get off the phone. I want to get to sleep by ten."

Jamie laughed, "It's only eight o'clock. You take more time to get ready for sleep than you do for going out."

I like to take lots of time to get ready for bed at night. While listening to calm music like Enya or Mozart, I perform my nighttime ritual. I climb into the bubble-filled bathtub, and when I finish soaking, I put on soothing lotion and slip into my favorite pajamas. Then I lie on my bed and write in my journal, or paint my toenails. By the time I am ready to go to sleep, I am relaxed and calm.

Perhaps a night ritual would be beneficial for you. Today, get your homework done early, hang up the telephone, and turn off the television. Give yourself time to take it easy and push all worries out of your mind. When you wake after giving yourself a night of pampering, you will feel energized and ready for the day ahead.

Time to Play

Playtime was probably what you thought about most as a child. Most likely, your favorite part of the school day was recess, and your biggest worry was what game you should play and whom to play it with. You had Barbies and board games. You played make-believe, rode your bike, and chased the ice cream truck down the street.

Somewhere along the line, play was exchanged for "maturity." Recess was taken over by more classes, and a stereo, computer, and telephone took the place of the toys that once filled your room. Suddenly the word *play* was gone from your vocabulary.

Maturity is good, but sometimes we can be too mature for our own good. In our desire to be cool and fit in, we have already forgotten (at age fourteen) the lesson we knew so well when we were six. Play is an enjoyable and essential part of life. Today, fly a kite, build a sand castle, run in the snow, or climb a tree. Cut loose, run free, and have fun!

You Are Not Inferior

One of my favorite quotes is from Eleanor Roosevelt: "No one can make you feel inferior without your consent." This is totally true. If you feel intimidated by someone, worry that nobody wants to be your friend, think that you aren't pretty, or believe that you are stupid and unathletic, it is because you have let someone or something convince you of this.

Today, make Eleanor Roosevelt's words your mantra; repeat them to yourself all day. Don't believe that you are worth less than your peers. Know in your heart that you are just as wonderful as everyone around you, and remember that the negative things people say about you will only affect you if you let them.

She's Such a . . .

Have you ever said, "Elizabeth is being a bitch!" or, "I hate Kari; she's such a slut"? These are harsh, strong statements, but sometimes we say these types of things without even thinking twice.

As girls, it is important that we help support *all* girls. Sure, you aren't going to like everyone or always agree with others' actions, and that's okay. Using words like *bitch*, *tramp*, *slut*, or *whore*, however, tells others that it is okay to view girls in this way. Even when said jokingly, these cut-downs are heavily loaded with negative connotations—they hurt all girls, not just the ones who are being directly insulted.

Today, quit using words that cut down girls and don't tolerate it when others use them.

Do What You Love

We live in a society where making money and becoming famous is seen as the ultimate success. We are told that if we study hard, get good grades, earn awards, and get recognized, we will be happy. Yet, most of the time we feel unsatisfied when we follow the path we "should" follow.

Today, do exactly what you love! Nothing will give your life more meaning than doing what *you* want to do, whether that is leaving public school to pursue your love of dance, or spending a semester in Germany on an exchange program.

Remember, the journey to happiness won't always be easy because it may mean going against your parents' hopes, or it may mean pursuing something that isn't seen as "valuable" by society. Keep in mind the famous words of Robert Frost: "I took the [road] less traveled by/And that has made all the difference." You are the only person who knows what will make you fulfilled, so follow *your* unique path.

Love What You Do

During my second year of cheerleading in high school, I started to wonder why I had tried out for the squad; it seemed like the downside to cheerleading outweighed the fun. "Everyone on the squad is so difficult," I would complain to my mom, "we spend all practice arguing about cheers and dances. I can't stand most of the girls, and I'm sick of basketball games. I hate it!"

My mother's simple question—"Why don't you quit?"—made me realize that I had control over my situation. Nobody was making me cheer; I chose to do it, and I could just as easily choose not to. I realized that I didn't want to quit, so I decided that I had better start loving cheer since *I* had made the choice to stay.

You always have a choice in life, and even if you can't change the situation that is bothering you, you can change your attitude about it. Life is precious. Today, start loving what you do.

Give 'Em Your Smile

Hate seems to be running rampant in our world today. The news is filled with stories about shootings in schools, racist and sexist acts, and domestic violence. Even starting rumors about people at school, glaring at someone you don't like, or thinking hateful thoughts about a person sends more hate out into the world.

People are starving for love, gentleness, and positive attention. You can do one simple thing to bring more kindness into this world: smile. It may not seem like much, but just remember how confident and cared about you feel when someone smiles at you.

Today, flash those pearly whites. Smile when you walk down the hallway—not just at the people you know, but at everyone. Popular or unpopular, older or younger, girl or guy—everyone benefits from a smile.

Popularity Does Not Equal Success

Popularity is a big deal for teens. For some reason we believe that popular people are somehow better than unpopular people. We forget that just because a person is popular and well known doesn't mean that he or she is well liked or successful.

Popular people don't always keep their "celebrity" status. After you graduate from high school, you will see that many of the popular people are headed nowhere as they enter their twenties. When you go back to your high school reunion, it might just be the "nerds" who are the most successful, most interesting people.

Madonna, a very successful performer, always says that she was totally unpopular in high school, and Bill Gates, one of the most successful men in the world, was probably not part of the "in" crowd. Today, remember that popularity doesn't mean anything in the big scheme of your life.

Are You Wearing **That?**

I'm sure this has happened to you: You're headed out the door to meet some friends when your mom raises one eyebrow, presses her lips together, and says, "Are you wearing *that?*" Whether it's ripped jeans, a tight halter top, or black pants, your mom may not always understand your clothing choices.

Today, make a clothing pact with your parents. Tell them that if they agree to let you choose what to wear when you go out with friends, then you will consult them on what to wear when you go out with them. With this agreement, they will know that when you are together, they won't feel uncomfortable about what you are wearing. It may seem a little unfair to let your parents have a say in what you wear, but if you are having clothing arguments with your parents, making this little compromise will make life much easier.

There Are No Quick Fixes

Life would be easy if you could fall asleep like Sleeping Beauty and awaken to a kiss from Prince Charming and a life of happily ever after. As you well know, life isn't a fairy tale. Life is hard. At times you are hurt and feel depressed. You will lose, get left out, make mistakes, and feel embarrassed.

Life is always a struggle with no quick fixes. The only way to get through hard times is to sit with your pain. When your boyfriend breaks up with you, let yourself cry and experience your broken heart instead of immediately try to find a new guy to fill his place. If you get cut from the soccer team, lose the election for class president, or get ditched by your best friends, be sad for awhile, and then accept these hurts as part of life.

Today, choose one thing that has been hard to get through and let yourself be sad, angry, or confused. Stop looking for a quick fix and accept the situation as it is.

I Can't Believe I Said That

"I can't believe you just said that!" Jenny's mouth hung open with amazement.

"What?" I asked.

"That was really mean thing to say about someone else," she replied. She was right. I was mean, but I was too embarrassed to admit it, so I just tried to defend myself.

Have you ever said something you knew wasn't the right thing to say once the words left your mouth? Maybe you let a secret slip, said something nasty about somebody, or told a little white lie that you knew would get you into even more trouble. The natural thing to do is to cover up your mistake by becoming defensive, arguing, "I didn't say that!" or, "You just took it the wrong way." Today, remember that the best thing to do in this situation is to take responsibility for your words by saying something like, "I'm sorry. I don't mean that, and I'm not even sure why I said it. I take it back."

Bye-Bye Values

"Do you want a beer, Amanda?" I turned around to find a gorgeous senior guy handing me a can of Budweiser. As I took the beer, I thought to myself, "What am I doing? I don't get drunk at parties. I don't even want to be seen with a beer in my hand."

Ignoring the thoughts running through my head, I forced the bitter liquid down my throat. "Disgusting!" I thought. "I'm not the type who gives into peer pressure. I should throw this out, and if someone else offers me a beer I'll say, 'No thanks. I don't drink'." Instead of following my own advice, I sat down on the couch next to the hot guy and took another sip.

Nobody is perfect. You can be smart, with high expectations for yourself, and still stray from your morals. Even if you believe strongly in your values, sometimes it is hard to stay true to them because you are learning about life as you grow. Just because you have messed up doesn't mean you have to give up. You are a healthy teenage girl learning about life through your experiences, so today, give yourself room to learn from your mistakes.

Contemplating Life's Essential Questions

Henry David Thoreau once said that he did "not want to live what is not life, life is so dear." What is "life"? What, to you, makes life worth living? Is there something that gets you going and fills your heart with joy? What do you yearn for? Does your life have a purpose? What goes into creating a truly happy life?

These are life's Essential Questions. Philosophers, artists, poets, and other great thinkers have debated them for thousands of years—they are not easily answered, but are definitely worth pondering. Thinking about these kinds of questions will challenge your mind and force you to examine your life and values.

Today, reflect on life's Essential Questions. What do *you* think is the meaning of life? Be thoughtful and reflective as you wrestle with this difficult idea. Contemplating life on a large level will help you discover what really matters to you.

Put an End to Rivalries

Girls are constantly in competition with each other, even if they're friends. In their fight for attention, praise, and popularity, girls gossip, stab each other in the back, and change their minds about whom they do and don't like at the drop of a hat.

Competing with your girlfriends defeats the purpose of friendship. If you are always trying to be better than your girlfriends, you will constantly bring them down instead of lifting them up. Competitions with friends may leave you feeling like your friends aren't your friends at all, but rather your enemies.

Today, when your friends do something well, congratulate them and be happy; don't try to compete with them. A supportive friend is the best kind of friend.

If You Don't Like Me for Me— Too Bad

Have you ever changed your personality to get a guy's attention? Pretended to like the music he loves or cut your hair a certain way because you heard him say he likes that style? Signed up for a class you know he's taking or told little lies to make him think the two of you have a lot in common?

Maybe you'll get his attention, but then what? A relationship can't go anywhere if you don't share common interests and values. No guy is worth the trouble of reinventing yourself. If he doesn't like you as you are, he isn't worth it. Today, instead of wasting your time and changing to fit a guy who isn't your match, put your energies into finding one who likes you for the way you really are.

Omigosh, Did You Hear?

Your best friend Nicole told you that she heard from her boyfriend, who heard from his friend Jake, who heard from his brother, who heard from your old friend Melanie, that your boyfriend is cheating on you!

Rumors travel fast and, like the messages in the game of telephone you played as a child, are completely distorted by the time they reach you. Some crucial words may be left out, and new ones may be added. People will misinterpret what they hear, and each will add their interpretation to the story to make it more interesting.

What you hear through the grapevine is never a completely true story. Today, if you hear something that upsets you, instead of believing it, go straight to the source. He or she will be able to clarify it better than any of the school gossips can.

You Are Creative, After All

Today, write a poem. Don't worry if you've never written a poem before or if you don't know the first thing about poetry. This is free poetry and there are no rules. All you have to do is let your creativity go wild.

A poem can be as simple as combining together some of your favorite words like this:

> Cool Blue
> Luscious Melody.

You can start a name poem by writing your name horizontally down the page. Use the letters in your name to create a poem this way:

> Always on the
> Move,
> Amanda
> Never stops performing
> Death-defying
> Acrobatics.

Poems don't have to make sense or have to rhyme. They can be silly or serious, real or make-believe. Today, play around with poetry and you'll be surprised to find that you are creative, after all.

In February. . .

Paint your nails red.

Make Valentine cookies and handmade cards to give to your friends and family on February 14.

If you don't have a special someone to spend Valentine's Day with, get together with a group of your single friends and have your own Valentine celebration.

Make a sachet for your drawers by wrapping some sweet-smelling potpourri in a piece of cloth and tying it with a ribbon.

Life Gets Better

When I was in high school, adults would scare me by telling me, "This is the best time of your life, so enjoy it!" "If this is the best time of my life," I would think to myself, "then I'm in trouble!"

I would like to disagree with these adults. I am in college now, and my life is *much* better than when I was a teen. Just as high school is better than junior high, college is better than high school—life gets better as you grow up. It is true that as you get older, your life becomes more complicated with more responsibilities, but what also comes with age are self-awareness and experience. As you grow, you grow into your true self and become more comfortable with who you are.

Today, when you are struggling, remember this: Your life will get much better!

Cherish Your Friendships

There is nothing like having close girlfriends. It is wonderful to have girls you can go to parties with, sit at home with, or cry to when you are feeling upset. You grow together and learn from each others' experiences. Some day you will look back on your life together and say, "Remember when. . . ?"

Enduring friendships make life rich, but they are rare. You're lucky if you have a close girlfriend because you don't often find someone you really connect with. It is important to cherish these friendships. Let your girlfriend know that you appreciate all she does for you. Today, drop a card in her locker that says, "Your friendship is important to me," or buy her a flower to say thanks. When you acknowledge the importance of the friends in your life, friendship bonds will grow deeper and last longer.

The Secret to Self-Esteem

What is self-esteem? Esteem means honor, respect, and admiration, so to have self-esteem means to honor, respect, and admire yourself.

There is a simple secret to attaining self-esteem — do the things that you tell yourself you are going to do. If you've always said that you're going to try out for the dance team, become a pianist, or start up a conversation with the guy you have a crush on, then trying out for the team, practicing piano every day, or saying hello to your dream boy will boost your self-esteem.

Today, pick something you've always said you wanted to try and do it. Regardless of whether you fail or succeed, doing what you've always wanted to do will show you that you can take risks and do what's in your heart. You will honor, respect, and admire yourself for following through on what you always said you would do.

They Make Me So Mad!

Your little brother spills paint all over your new sweater; a friend copies your homework, and you get in trouble for cheating; you discover that your boyfriend kissed a girl from another school. You want to scream, and it's all their fault! They make you so mad!

Before you run off into a fit of rage, think again. *You*, and only you, are in control of your feelings. *They* didn't make you mad; *you* chose to be mad about what they did. It is true that you don't have control over the actions of others, but you do have a lot of control over your own emotions. As the German philosopher Goethe said, "In all situations, it is my response that decides whether a crisis will be escalated or de-escalated. . . ."

Today, remember that the way you react to something is completely your choice.

Think Before You React

When someone does something that upsets you, your first response is to get mad. It's easy to blow up and yell when someone upsets you. It is harder, yet much more mature and productive, to think before you react.

Today, instead of instantly reacting with anger, ask yourself, "What is the best way to handle this situation? How can I turn this negative event into a positive one?" Your first impulse may be to scream at your little brother after he spilt paint on your sweater, but a better response might be to tell him that he shouldn't use paint around your clothes, and then keep your clothes out of his reach. Explain to your friend why you were upset that you got in trouble when she copied your homework. Break up with your cheating boyfriend by calmly telling him you don't date guys who cheat. Not only will these tactics force other people to see their mistakes, they will help you feel a lot better because you didn't just react out of anger. When you get mad, you are the one who suffers— anger burns inside of you, consumes your thoughts, and puts you in a bad mood.

Listen to Your Intuition Talking

Once, I met a guy from another school at a party. Although he had a cute smile, was easy to talk to, and we really hit it off, something deep inside of me told me he couldn't be trusted. However, I ignored my gut instincts, only to find out four months later that he had been cheating on me the entire time we'd been dating. If I had paid attention to my initial intuition, I would have saved myself a lot of heartache.

With practice, you can learn how to read the signs your intuition sends you. Today, pay attention to what your instincts tell you throughout the day. Do you feel a knot in your stomach? Does your heart ache? If so, you aren't making the right decision. You will know you are doing the right thing if you feel energized and at peace. Be aware of the ways your intuition communicates with you, and follow its advice.

Living the Golden Rule

"Treat others as you want to be treated." You know the golden rule, but have you ever thought about what it really means? How *do* you want to be treated? Do you want people to say nasty things about you behind your back, spread rumors about you, or ignore you because they think you're a nerd? Do you want people to judge you, make fun of you, lie to you, yell at you, or hurt you? Probably not. You want to be treated lovingly, with kindness, and every person you interact with wants to be treated that way too.

It takes practice to make the golden rule a part of your daily life, so today, make a conscious effort to treat others with authentic warmth. As Mother Teresa said, "Be the living expression of God's kindness: kindness in your face, kindness in your eyes, kindness in your smile."

Kiss Me

"I bet it's going to happen tonight!" My best friend was bouncing with excitement.

"What is?" I asked.

"Jeremy is going to kiss you!"

I was shocked, "You mean French kiss? At the movies?"

I wasn't as excited about this whole kissing idea as my friend was. She had already Frenched three guys; I hadn't kissed anyone and wasn't particularly eager to start just yet. Jeremy and I had only been together for a few weeks, but I felt pressured to "catch up" with my peers. After the movie that night, I did have my first experience with the infamous "French kiss."

"How was it?" my friends asked, anxiously awaiting my reply.

"Great!" I lied. In reality, it was disgusting, and I couldn't understand why anyone would actually like to kiss that way. I hated it, and didn't try it again for a long time after that.

Kissing and other stuff is fun, but you don't need to keep up with your friends' experiences. Today, remember that you are your own person—follow your own schedule and your *own* comfort level.

Getting Lost

So, maybe you've made some big mistakes in your life or have taken taken a few wrong paths, and now your life has turned into something much different than what you had wished for. Maybe you're failing your classes, did something to lose your parents' trust, had sex with someone and then regretted it, or started smoking, drinking, or using drugs.

Everybody makes decisions they regret at some point in their lives; the people who succeed are those who realize that every mistake is an opportunity to learn. Instead of dwelling on the bad things you have done, remember that it's never too late to create the life you really want. Today, forgive yourself for mistakes, don't give up, and know that your life is worth saving.

I Need Help

Do you ever have problems that your friends don't understand or that you can't talk about with your parents? Maybe you're feeling depressed and don't know why, or you're doing poorly in school and can't bring your grades up. Maybe you're pregnant or are abusing drugs.

It is always okay to ask for help when you need it. When you get a broken leg or an ear infection, you go to a doctor. It's just as important to get help with your emotional hurts. Talk to a school counselor or a pastor at your church; these people are trained to listen and help you solve your problems. If they can't help you, they'll be able to refer you to someone who can.

Today, remember that asking for help with your emotional struggles doesn't make you a weird or helpless person. Getting help shows that you care about yourself and want to take action to live happily. We all need a little assistance getting back on the right track at times.

Flying to the Sun

According to classical mythology, Icarus was a boy whose father made wings out of wax and feathers so that the two of them could fly to a new land. Ignoring his father's warnings about flying too high, Icarus flew up to the sun. The heat melted his wings, and before he could make it safely to land, Icarus fell into the sea and drowned.

Sure, Icarus didn't make it across the water, but think of the experience he had! Icarus flew, saw the sun up close, and glided with clouds; for a moment he was a bird!

Being victorious doesn't always mean coming in first place; sometimes the glory is in the journey. Maybe you lost the election for school secretary, but having to give a speech in front of the whole school cured your fear of public speaking. Maybe you didn't get an A in English, but you still discovered during the semester that you loved Shakespeare. Maybe you and your boyfriend broke up, but you got to experience love and now have many fond memories.

Today, when you feel like a flop, remember Icarus. Some falls are not failures; they are endings to wonderful triumphs.

I Can't Date Him, He's Too...

You've heard it before and have probably complained about it yourself: "There are no good guys around!" We girls like to gripe and moan that all guys are jerks, have big egos, or are confusing. Even when we finally discover a nice guy, we find faults in him—he's too short, too tall, too nice, doesn't like to talk on the phone, or doesn't know how to dance. And you think *guys* are picky?

If you're constantly whining about not having a boyfriend, maybe it's time to look at how you're judging guys. It's good to set high standards when it comes to boys, but high doesn't mean impossible. Today, remember that you should get to know as many guys as you can, so be open to different types. You may be surprised—a guy who isn't "your type" may turn out to be the guy you really fall for. Even if he doesn't become your boyfriend, he might make a great boy *friend*. Meeting many different types of guys will help you figure out what qualities you want in a guy and what kinds of guys you like to be around.

Why Don't You Trust Me?

"I told my mom that I didn't sneak out last weekend and she doesn't believe me," I complained to my friend.

"Why should she believe you? You did sneak out," she answered.

"Yeah, but she doesn't know that because she was visiting my grandma. I can't believe she doesn't trust me!"

Before you get mad because your parents don't trust you, ask yourself this question: "Am I being trustworthy?" With all the new freedom you push for, your parents are bound to worry. Many times parents become overprotective and untrusting because they don't know how to deal with their nervous reaction when you ask to stay out later, go to parties, or date.

Today, ease your parents' worries by showing that you can be trusted. Come home when you say you will, call them to check in during the night, and give them the number of where you're going so that they can reach you if they need to. It's simple: If you act trustworthy, your parents will be more likely to give you the freedom you want.

Spread the Love

If love makes life wonderful, then why are many people depressed on Valentine's Day? Your heart should be full of joy on the day of love. Instead, February 14 is usually a reminder of your not-so-great romantic life. You may feel undesirable when you remember the boyfriend who broke up with you for another girl or lonely because you've never had one "true love."

Before you get down in the dumps, remember that love doesn't just come in the form of a boyfriend. There are many types of love — love for your parents, your siblings, your girlfriends, your guy friends, your pets, or your stuffed animals. You love to swim, to read, to play music, or to cook. On this Valentine's Day, bask in all the love that surrounds you. Focus your attention on everything you love, and give love to others who need it. When you give attention to the love you have instead of the love you are lacking, your life, heart, and spirit will be happy!

Everyone Thinks I Am Pretty

I didn't think I was pretty as a teen. I longed to be tall, with long blonde hair and tan skin. When I walked down the halls, I wanted guys to turn their heads. But I never grew past five feet, my white skin only turned red when I went into the sun, and I never saw any guys turn around when I passed. "I'm so ugly," I would say. "I want to be one of those girls who is so gorgeous that guys talk about how pretty I am when I'm not around." I failed to realize that maybe guys *were* talking about me when I wasn't around, but I never knew because I wasn't around.

Stop convincing yourself that you aren't attractive. Remember, everyone may think that you are the prettiest girl in the world, but you may never know because they may not ever tell you.

You are beautiful! Today, instead of telling yourself that everyone thinks you're ugly, tell yourself that everyone thinks you are pretty. Open your eyes and let yourself see that people around you think you are beautiful.

Why Did You Do That to Me?

How do you feel when you hear that somebody has been spreading lies about you, when your friend goes after the boy she knows you like, or when the person you confided in spills your big secret?

When someone hurts me, my first reaction is to get revenge. I want to talk about that person behind her back, or reveal secrets that she has told me. If I make her look bad, I can regain my good image and patch up the hurt she caused me, right?

Wrong! You won't feel better about yourself by bringing someone else down; you will only make yourself feel worse. When someone hurts you, it's important to be the bigger person. Confront your friend and ask her why she acted the way she did. Did you do something to make her mad? What made her turn against you like that? Today, instead of immediately seeking revenge, confront the person who has hurt you. You'll feel better.

A Prayer for All Things

Make this Buddhist prayer your wish for today.

> May I be happy;
> May I be peaceful;
> May I be free.
>
> May my friends be happy;
> May my friends be peaceful;
> May my friends be free.
>
> May my enemies be happy;
> May my enemies be peaceful;
> May my enemies be free.
>
> May all things be happy;
> May all things be peaceful;
> May all things be free.

Keep this prayer in your heart and recite it to yourself throughout the day. When you pray for happiness, peace, and freedom for all people, you will bring these things to yourself and others.

Singing the Blahs

"I'm bored!!!" I grumbled through my clenched teeth.

"Well," my mother said, "you could empty the dishwasher or clean out the hall closet. I know you haven't finished your science project, and your laundry needs to be folded and put away."

"Yeah right," I replied, "just the thought of doing those makes me even more bored."

It's the blahs. Those times when life feels completely unexciting—when you are uninspired, uninterested, unmotivated, and dull. You need a change of pace. No matter who you are, there will always be blah times in your life. You will still find yourself getting bored when you are twenty-one, or even if you move to a bigger, more exciting city.

Today, chase away the blahs with an anti-blah list. Write down things that excite you, things you love to do, and things you hope to do someday. When you feel a case of the blahs coming on, take out your list and pick something to do. Soon life will excite you once more.

Do It Now

"Amanda," my mom said, "will you please get your books out of the hallway? Grandma's coming over tonight, so I need you to help me get the house clean."

"I'll do it later," I said, hoping she'd leave me alone. I was in no mood to be nagged.

"I need you to do it now so that I can vacuum."

"Mom, I'll do it, just wait a few minutes. I'm in the middle of something."

"It will only take you one minute, and then you can go back to what you are doing," she argued.

"Calm down! I'll do it. You don't have to be so demanding," I yelled as I stomped out of the room.

Today, when your parents ask you to help them around the house, do it right away. You will avoid unnecessary arguments, and it is much quicker and easier to clean your dishes, take out the garbage, or hang up your coat right away than it is to argue about it for ten minutes. Watch how much smoother your relationship with your parents can be when you say, "I'll do it now."

Celebrate Those Who Have Died

When a family member or a close friend dies, you may feel like part of you has died along with that person. It's hard to think about the person without getting upset, and things that they did that used to make you smile now bring you to tears.

Memories of a loved one you have lost can be painful. Yet May Sarton had it right when she said, "What is there to do when people die—people so dear and rare—but bring them back by remembering?"

Today, remember a loved one who has died by writing down your memories, the special bonds you shared, the fun times you had together, and the things he or she taught you about life. Make a special scrapbook with your memories, pictures, quotes, artwork, and poetry, and dedicate it to that person. When you celebrate the life of a person who has passed away, you help the healing process and keep his or her spirit strong and alive.

A Girl's Best Friend

My cat always knows when I'm upset. She senses my pain and jumps onto my bed when I cry, nestling next to me as she watches me, her expression saying, "Everything will be okay, Amanda." She obviously loves me, and she takes care of me just as much as I take care of her.

Pets are the most loyal of friends. They listen to you talk about your problems for hours without telling any of your secrets. Treat them well, and they will always be excited to see you.

Today, show your pets how much you appreciate their company.

Try Something New

"You should sign up for a painting class, Amanda," my English teacher said to me.

Shocked, I replied, "What? Are you joking? I can't paint!"

"Just try it," she encouraged. "You might discover something about yourself."

She was right! I discovered I love to paint. The feel of the brush dipping into the paint, the gentle glide of my wrist as I decorated the canvas, and the rich colors that filled my eyes all spoke to my heart. I found myself spending hours after school working in the art room. Painting left me feeling relaxed, and it was a wonderful way to escape from the gossip, homework, sadness, and other stresses of life.

Today, take a step toward discovering something that ignites your creativity. Try different activities until you find one that sparks your interest—go to an art museum, take piano lessons, write poetry, dance, try out for a play, learn to design houses, or plant a garden. You are full of artistic abilities; just give your creative side a chance to show itself.

When Boyfriends Come before Best Friends

"I've got to get off the phone with you," Liz said after she clicked over from answering the other line. "That's Blake."

I was hurt, but I wasn't surprised. Blake was Liz's new boyfriend, and he had bumped me from being best friend to only-needed-when-boyfriend-isn't-around friend. I said I was happy for her, and I mostly was, but part of me couldn't wait for them to break up so I could have my best friend back.

Girls always seem to put their girlfriends on the back burner when a guy comes around. Today, if you have a friend who has ditched you for her boyfriend, let her know you are hurt. Tell her you're happy for her, but that you miss having her around, and you wish that she would keep time for your friendship. If she doesn't change, maybe she isn't that great of a friend anyway. Remember, you deserve to have friends who keep you in their lives regardless of their relationship status.

Pinch Your Pennies

I have a piggy bank where I keep all my change. Whenever I find change in my wallet or sitting in my desk drawers, I immediately put it into my bank. When the piggy bank is full, I empty it out, put my change into coin rollers from the bank, and head for the bank to exchange my quarters, dimes, nickels, and pennies for dollars.

Change adds up sooner than you think. My friend once went around school and asked everyone to donate a little bit of change for his ski trip, and after a few weeks, he had enough money to pay for more than half of his trip!

Today, start pinching your pennies. You'll be excited when you see your change become dollars.

Feel Your Spirit

I often felt bad as a teen because my family didn't go to church regularly. Even though we celebrated Christmas, I didn't really consider myself a Christian and would wonder, "What religion am I?" I knew that I believed in God, angels, and spirits because I often felt their presence in my life, but I wasn't sure how to put my beliefs into words.

You don't have to be religious to be spiritual. Spirit is everywhere—in people and in animals. Some Native American tribes believe that plants, rocks, water, and other parts of nature have spirit. Spirituality is hard to explain; you can't touch it, but it surrounds you every day. Don't worry if you can't verbalize all of your beliefs or feelings about your religion and spirit—these things are not easy to put into words. You feel your spirit when something touches you so deeply it moves you to tears, when you are so excited you get goose bumps, or when you are just happy to be alive. Today, be aware that spirit is something that cannot be rationalized, but it can be felt by every person.

Promise You Won't Tell

"I have to tell you something, but you have to promise that you won't tell anyone," your friend says to you. A secret is coming—classified information just for you. "I won't tell anyone," you say. Yet after your friend tells the secret, do you keep your promise, or do you immediately run to share the juicy information you just heard?

The temptation to share your classified information can be overwhelming, but think of how you would feel if someone told a secret of yours. You may not think that the secret is that big of a deal, but people are sensitive about different things. Maybe your friend told you that she likes a guy named Brian, but she doesn't want you to tell anyone. If you aren't afraid to let guys know when you like them, you may not find your friend's secret worth keeping. Today, if someone asks you to keep a secret, be a good friend and do as they ask.

Get Along with the Folks

Parents can be difficult. They make ridiculous rules, are embarrassing, yell for no reason, and snoop into your private life—it can often seem that your parents are more trouble than they are worth. Wouldn't life be simpler if you didn't have to worry about them?

In the story of "Hansel and Gretel," the two children run away from home to escape their seemingly evil parents only to find themselves in a worse predicament with an evil witch. When they finally escape, they realize that life with their parents isn't as bad as they had originally thought.

Today, make an effort to get along with your parents. Do whatever it takes, because when you have a good relationship with your parents, you will also have their support, and that will make everything else in your life easier to handle.

Keep Your Teddy Bears

Every girl has a stuffed animal, favorite pillow, or little blanket that she's had since childhood. No matter how tattered and dirty it is, it soothes you with its smell of home. As we get older, we become a little embarrassed by our childhood comforts. Whenever I went to slumber parties, I would always bring my favorite teddy bear with me, keeping him hidden away in my sleeping bag so that nobody would make fun of me for bringing a stuffed animal.

Hold on to your childhood comforts. My teddy bear has been on just about every vacation I've ever taken and has soaked up the tears from my many broken hearts. It isn't immature to keep these things — when I arrived at college, I noticed that every girl, and even some guys, had old stuffed animals on their beds to comfort them during difficult times.

Seize Today

What better day to live Horace's famous words, "Seize the day," than today, leap year? This is a rare day, perfect for rare opportunities. It won't come again for four years, so make it a day that you do something extraordinary, something you haven't yet had the courage to do.

Talk to the boy you've had a crush on all year, go out for the track team like you've always said you would, get rid of a friend who has been bringing you down—it's time to stop thinking about it and go for it. Seize today! You have nothing to lose.

In March. . .

Suggest that your family go out for dinner at a restaurant you've never been to. Try Greek, Indian, or Thai food. Go out for sushi, or go to the new pizza restaurant that just opened up down the street.

Wear green on St. Patrick's Day, March 17. Get decked out in an all-green outfit, or simply tie a green bow in your hair and put a clover sticker on your cheek.

Wear perfume or a sweet-smelling lotion, and get excited about the coming of spring.

The Out-of-the-Ordinary Month

March has always been one of my least favorite months. It is the month of the doldrums. Whenever March rolls around, I cringe, envisioning four straight weeks with absolutely nothing new or exciting happening. During March, I complain about the rain in Seattle, become bored with my friends, and dream of moving to a tropical paradise.

Make March Out-of-the-Ordinary Month. Spice up your usual routine by filling every weekend with fun activities for you and your friends, making new outfits from your old wardrobe, cutting your hair, listening to music that makes you excited, and rearranging your bedroom. When the humdrum of everyday life gets you down, it's up to you to create the fun.

Friends Who Pull You Down

In junior high, my girlfriends and I would all spend Friday nights together. Our slumber parties started out as innocent girl bonding, but over time, they turned into vicious gossip-fests. We said mean things about everyone we knew, and it got so bad that I was afraid to miss one of the slumber parties for fear of becoming the target of the night's gossip.

I always thought of myself as the girl who didn't say bad things about people, but as soon as I got to one of these parties, I jumped right in. I always felt guilty the next day, and slowly I began to realize that these girls were bringing out the worst in me.

Sometimes we get so caught up in wanting to be liked that we hang out with people who pull us down. If you find you do things with your friends that go against your morals or change your personality, it might be time for you to find a new group. Your friends should bring out your best qualities, and you should never feel less than your best self when you are with them.

Losing Bad Friends

Have you ever found yourself with a friend whom you don't feel good about? Maybe she puts you down, pressures you into doing things that make you uncomfortable, is overbearing, or isn't honest. Maybe she's a bad influence, a backstabber, or maybe you are just growing apart. Pulling away from a friend is a hard thing to do, but if you are in a negative situation, finding new friends will make you happiest in the long run.

Instead of suddenly dropping your old friend, ease your way out of that friendship and into new ones. Start getting to know new girls from your classes or sports teams. Invite them to hang out with you sometime. You don't have to stop hanging out with your old friend, but you should start spending more time with others. If you keep in contact with your old friend and break the bonds slowly, you will avoid hurt feelings and unnecessary fights. Soon you will find yourself in a friendship situation that is more positive.

It's Great to Be Alive

Today is a wonderful day! That's right—you have an amazing day ahead, full of opportunity, happiness, fun, and excitement. "What?" you ask. "It's raining out, I have two tests, my throat is sore, and I just had a fight with my mom. Today sucks."

You're wrong. Today *is* a great day. For each negative in your life, there are just as many positives—they may just be harder for you to see right now. No matter what, you can be happy if you focus on the positives instead of the negatives.

Today, stop emphasizing all the negatives in your life. Positives don't have to be phenomenal events; small positives are just as important. Be happy because your mom packed a delicious sandwich for lunch, because they played your favorite song on the radio on your way to school, because your friends made you laugh, or because you know that there are many wonderful things waiting to happen to you.

Follow Your Own Leader

You know the story "The Emperor's New Clothes." The vain emperor, whose only concern in life is to have the best clothes by the most popular designers, hires two scoundrels posing as tailors who sew him clothes using "invisible, magic fabric." When the emperor parades down the street in his new clothes, nobody can see his clothes, but they don't want to look stupid, so they all pretend they can. Finally a young boy who isn't concerned about fitting in stands up and yells, "The emperor has no clothes!"

At times we pretend or go against our own beliefs to avoid being weird or different from our peers. We follow along mindlessly, without noticing that what we are saying and doing is stupid or wrong. The people in "The Emperor's New Clothes" were afraid of looking stupid, but by pretending to see clothes that weren't even there, they only made themselves look more stupid. Remember, the majority isn't always right. Be courageous today and follow your heart, what you know deep down to be true.

I'm So Busy
I'm Going to Explode!

Ahhhhh! Two tests, a paper due tomorrow, a speech to give at the upcoming assembly, community service for honor society, a track meet, baby-sitting on Thursday, and you promised a friend you'd help her study for her Spanish test on Friday. You've got too much to do and not enough time to get it done.

It's great to be involved and work hard, but there's a point when you have spread yourself too thin. When you break down in tears because you are feeling stressed, don't have time to sit down for dinner, or can't sleep at night because you are worrying about everything you have to do, you have taken on too much.

Today, slow down. Cut some things from your "must-do" list. It's okay to admit that you have taken on too much. You are still a hard worker, and you will still get into a good college, I promise. Give yourself time to enjoy the activities you are doing instead of constantly worry about what you have to do next. It's much better to do a few things wholeheartedly than a bunch of them halfheartedly.

Learning to Pray

"There is no life without prayer. Without prayer there is only madness and horror," said Vasili Rozanov. It is true; prayer has the power to bring gentleness and hope into the world like nothing else.

"But I don't know how to pray," you say. Maybe you worry that prayer is only for religious people or that you won't pray correctly. Prayers are used for many things, and there really is no wrong way to pray. We pray for answers to life's questions, we pray to give thanks, or we pray to ask for help for people we care about. You can pray to God, or to your grandmother who passed away. You can pray to the universe, to a tree, or you can sit quietly and pray to your own inner spirit.

Today, take ten minutes of quiet time for prayer. You don't have to be part of any particular religion or get down on your knees. All you need is a thought, a hope, a fear, or an appreciation that you would like to share.

I'm Being Outgrown by a Friend

In seventh grade, my best friend and I were inseparable. People called us twins because we spent every minute together and we looked alike. I admired her, trusted her, and had more fun with her than with anyone else. I thought we'd be friends forever. Then one day, everything changed. She stopped asking me to hang out and didn't return my calls. I was devastated, and for the first time, I felt like an outsider looking in on her life. I cried and longed to have her back, but she didn't seem to even notice that I was missing from her life.

Sometimes your friends will outgrow you before you outgrow them. Losing a friend is a painful feeling, but remember that this does not mean you're a bad person, a loser, or boring. People change without warning, and that isn't your fault. Be gentle with yourself during times of breaking friendships, and know that you will soon find a new friend who will be just right for who you are now.

Dealing with Parents' Problems

We count on our parents to provide us with food, protect us from the harsh world, help us when we have problems, and tell us everything we need to know to survive. Children often view their parents as perfect, saintlike beings. Now that you are older, you may see your parents in a clearer light, and you may realize that they are not perfect.

One of the hardest things to do is admit that your parents have problems. It is extremely disheartening when you realize that your parents are not the superhuman beings you once saw them to be. You may find yourself feeling guilty for your parents' shortcomings and want to solve all of their problems.

You need to realize that your parents' problems are not your fault. Even if you were the perfect angel child, your parents would still have gotten a divorce, your mom would still be an alcoholic, your dad would still yell. Don't feel guilty—your parents' problems have to do with something that is going on inside of them, not you.

Let's Talk about Sex

Sex is everywhere. You see it on television and in movies, you hear about it on the radio, and you read about it in magazines and books. It's a normal topic of conversation among teenagers. You've probably been in conversations where people discussed how far they'd gone, who was a good kisser, what guys they wanted to "get on," and what couples were "doing it." These conversations are normal, and you probably don't think twice when talking about these things.

It's time to start thinking twice, because sex is going to be our main topic for the next seven days. Pay attention to the way sex is talked about and portrayed in your everyday life. Notice how your peers talk about it. Listen for sexual jokes and casual remarks. What do you see on TV and in magazines or books? Watch closely; listen closely. Are you surprised? Offended? Uncomfortable? Pay attention because during these next few days, you are going to closely examine and define your values on sex.

I'm Not a Prude!

"Are you a prude, Amanda?" Ian asked me at a party where everyone was playing "Spin the Bottle."

"Umm, no," I answered. I had no idea what "prude" meant but by the way he said it, I knew it was not the cool thing to be.

"Have you French kissed before?"

"Yes," I said.

"How many guys?" he asked.

"Three," I lied. The truth was zero.

"Good," he said approvingly. "You aren't a prude then."

I always felt so ashamed of my sexual inexperience. I felt bad that I hadn't kissed a lot of guys, or when I didn't understand all of the sexual jokes my friends made. I thought that if I didn't go "far enough," I must be unattractive and slow in some way.

It's hard to find a balance when it comes to getting physical. If you do too much, you are considered a slut, but if you move too slowly, you are called a prude. Remember, you never need to feel ashamed of being behind your friends. Move at your own pace, and eventually you will figure it all out. Do only what makes *you* feel comfortable, and never, ever, anything more.

Be Picky

Teenage boys are very interested in sex—they talk about it, dream about it, read about it, and want it. Some guys will say and do just about anything to get you to make out and have sex with them, so it's up to you to protect your body.

Don't let just anyone touch you, kiss you, or flirt with you. Be picky. Set high standards and make guys meet them before you become physically involved with them. Many girls think that as long as they aren't having sex, it's okay to do anything with just about anybody. However, it's best to care about your body, and that includes making the guys you are involved with care about it, too. A good guy won't try to take advantage of you or ask you to do anything you aren't comfortable with.

Make guys show you respect before you let them touch you. He should return your phone calls, talk to you at school, make an effort to see you on the weekends, ask you about your day, give you sincere compliments, and make you feel good about yourself. Make sure he's interested in *all* of you.

Are You Ready?

Before you jump into a sexual relationship, think about the different aspects of sex. Do you feel comfortable talking to your partner about birth control? Are you comfortable going into a store and buying condoms? Are you positive that your boyfriend will be faithful to you? Have you two been dating for longer than six months? Would your boyfriend support you if you got pregnant? Do you and your partner discuss your fears, worries, hopes, and other feelings about sex? Are you comfortable with your body and with being naked in front of your boyfriend? Are you 100 percent positive 100 percent of the time that you are ready to have sex? If you cannot answer every one of these questions with a definite "yes," you may want to rethink your decision.

Sex is not evil, wrong, or taboo, but it *is* risky. Sex can be wonderful and intimate, but *only* when it is shared between two people who truly love each other and who have taken the time to discuss all the factors, both physical and emotional, that go into taking such a big step.

Sex Is Complicated

Sex is not simply about intercourse. Sex is complicated. There are emotional aspects—the sadness that comes with losing your virginity, the fear of what your partner is thinking, and the extra devastation if the two of you break up. You have to worry about birth control—who is going to buy the condom and what happens if it breaks? Don't forget about STDs—even if your partner has only had sex with one other person besides you, he is still at risk. There is always the final question—where are you going to do it? You'll have to sneak around parents, find empty bedrooms at parties, or park the car in a deserted parking lot. Sex doesn't sound as simple as it once did, does it?

When you are thinking about having sex, take this into consideration: Many of my friends and older women have said to me, "I wish I had waited to have sex." I have never heard anyone say, "I shouldn't have waited. I wish I'd had sex earlier." Think about the complications that sex will add to your life before you make your decision.

Waiting Isn't Easy

By the time I was eighteen, many of my friends were sexually active, and some had already had several different partners. Seeing so many people around me having sex left me wondering, "What's the big deal? Why am I waiting if it's so normal for everyone else?"

Sexual pressure is everywhere. Friends talk about sex like it's the greatest thing they've ever done, your boyfriend tells you he's ready to "take your relationship to the next level," and you see teens on television and in movies doing it. When you're in a serious relationship with a guy you love, the temptation to have sex can be even greater.

Deciding to wait for sex or choosing not to have any more partners until you are older doesn't end the difficulty of dealing with sexual pressures. You will continually be tempted, and you may waver on your decision to wait. Promise yourself that any judgments you make about sex will only happen after you have taken the time to think over the pros and cons. Don't make a decision in the heat of the moment. The more you stick by your decision, the stronger you will become in your resolution.

Desires Aren't Bad

Many adults feel uncomfortable with teenagers' sexuality. They aren't quite sure how to talk to us about it, or how to show us the best way to deal with our feelings. Often adults preach at us, telling us that sex is taboo and that sexual feelings are bad. We are told to repress our desires and feel ashamed about our thoughts.

Sexuality is a wonderful thing. You don't have to feel uncomfortable that you are curious about sex, want to become a good kisser, or like to make out—it's natural. It's important for you to allow yourself to feel. Remember that feeling comfortable with your desires doesn't mean acting on all of them. Learn how to deal with your uncertainty and excitement about sex in a healthy way. Kiss the boy you have a crush on, but don't rush into the bedroom with him on your first date just because you are curious.

There's a fine line between acting on your sexual desires in a beneficial way and going too far too fast. Take things slowly. Do what is best for you, both mentally and physically. Try to understand and become comfortable with your desires before you act on them.

For a Good Time, Keep Your Clothes On

When I ask teenage girls why they have sex with guys, many of them respond, "It's fun," or, "It's a way to show someone that you like them." True, but there are many other ways to do both of these things.

Picture your idea of a perfect day spent with a guy. What types of things does it entail? Maybe it's dinner on the beach, or a day of skiing, or hanging out renting movies and eating pizza together.

Relationships grow stronger through shared experiences, and if your relationship revolves around getting it on, you have a problem. Make a list of fun things you want to do with your boyfriend, when you go out on a date with a guy, or when you are out with a group of guys and girls.

Watch how much closer you become by doing all sorts of fun things together. You will quickly discover which guys are worth keeping around because they are excited about going out and having a good time, and you will weed out the ones who only want to kiss and run.

What I Think about Sex

Today, think about your values regarding sex and make a commitment to yourself. What you write doesn't have to be just about intercourse; it can be about whatever things you're dealing with right now—kissing, making out, or even flirting.

In your journal, write out your commitment. Maybe it's, "I will only kiss boys who have shown they respect me and whom I've been dating for at least a month," or, "I'm going to withhold from having sex until I've graduated from high school and am in a serious relationship." List the reasons why you made this decision. Maybe you don't feel comfortable doing anything more than kissing boys, or you aren't having sex because you worry about getting pregnant. Any reason is a good reason.

Throughout your life, you will be faced with new challenges regarding sex. By revising and updating your commitment, you can feel happy with the sexual decisions you are making and you will be confident that you will be able to keep the resolutions you have made.

Cry to Me

What do you do when your friends come to you to cry? Most of us try to cheer them up. We say things like, "Don't worry, everything will be okay." We try to get their minds off their sadness by making them laugh or by changing the subject. When we see friends in pain, we want to stop the bad feelings as quickly as possible. However, our good intentions aren't necessarily helpful.

As backward as it may seem, the best thing you can do for your friend is to encourage her tears. Tell her, "It's good for you to cry, you know. Keep crying." It can be uncomfortable to watch a friend cry because it reminds us of our own sadness. Let your friend feel her sadness and get all her emotions out before you try to cheer her up. Not only will your friend's hurt heal faster when you encourage her to feel her pain, but you will feel more comfortable doing the same for yourself the next time you need a good cry.

None of Your Business

I had a friend in high school who was always worrying about what other people thought of her. She would always ask me, "Does Stephanie like me? What did Kevin say about me?" I would tell her nothing but the good things that others said about her just to save her feelings. I knew she would be devastated if she thought someone didn't like her, so I decided that a little white lie would spare her feelings.

What I learned from the experience is that what other people think of you is none of your business. People will pretend they like you even if they don't, or they may seem to hate you but are really just quiet. No matter how hard you try, you will never *really* know what others truly think, so it is a waste of time to try to find out. Even if you were to find out what someone else thinks of you, why does it really matter? The truth is that the only opinion that matters is your own.

Turning Defeats into Victories

By this point in your life, you are well aware of the fact that life isn't fair. That still doesn't keep you from wondering, "Why is life so hard for me?"

Life is a struggle for everyone. If you try to escape from your hardships—by turning to drugs, food, alcohol, or sex—they will destroy you and turn you into a weak, angry person. If you turn to face your hardships, they turn you into a stronger, happier person.

Today, ask yourself, "What can I do to turn my hardships into positive experiences?" Maybe an alcoholic parent has caused a lot of pain in your life. You could volunteer at a center for children of alcoholics, or help others through your experience by writing a book about how you have dealt with it.

Get a Job

What are you going to do for summer vacation? Have you thought about getting a job? That's right—work! You may think March is too early to start planning for summer, but many places start hiring for the summer about now.

The types of jobs available for teens are endless. You could work at a restaurant, a clothing store, or a day camp for kids. These aren't the only options. Be creative. My grandmother is always looking for teenagers to wash her car once a week. Maybe you know an elderly lady who could use some help. Find someone who needs a baby-sitter for the summer. Train to be a lifeguard and spend your summer at the local pool. Offer to mow your neighbors' lawns or walk their dogs. Deliver pizzas or drive an ice cream truck.

Today, keep your mind open to job ideas for this summer. It's never too early to get information.

Impress the Boss

Working at The Gap had been a dream of mine. It seemed like a fun, upbeat environment, but I knew they didn't hire anyone under sixteen. The spring after my sixteenth birthday, I went in and picked up an application. The manager said that they weren't hiring right then, but to call back in May. When I called in May, they said to call again in June. When I called in June, they told me to try again in two weeks. I called two weeks later and finally got an interview. The managers were impressed with my persistence because it was obvious that I wanted to work, and I finally got the job!

Sometimes looking for a job is discouraging. Managers can be intimating and give you the run-around but, in the end, persistence pays off. Employers want people who are enthusiastic, responsible, and excited about the job.

If there is someplace that you really want to work, get in there and show them that you want it. Call, drop in, call back; you are building a relationship with the employer. When they see that you are serious about working, they are more likely to hire you!

Rolling in the Dough

You may have noticed that life gets more expensive as you get older. It can be a pain depending on your parents for all the things you want. If you get a job this summer, you will have more financial freedom.

Before you start working, it's a good idea to plan how you will spend your money. Open a bank account, or use a piggy bank, and promise to save a certain amount of each paycheck. Maybe you want to stick half of your paycheck in the bank while spending the other half on clothes, hanging out with friends, and other expenses. My friend saved a little bit of all the money she ever got—birthday and Christmas money in addition to what she earned working. As soon as she turned sixteen, she had enough money to buy a car.

While it is nice to have money to spend, it is even nicer to have money to save.

Lose Gracefully

You tried out for the soccer team and got cut; you didn't get the lead role in the school play; the guy you have a crush on is going out with somebody else. You've lost out on something you wanted, and you're upset and a little down on yourself.

You've probably heard the rule about being a good sport when you lose. Everyone loses sometimes; this just happens to be your time. Be a graceful loser, and remember that there are many wins in store for you. Putting down the coach of the soccer team or cutting down the girl who beat you out for the play will only keep you feeling bad and make you look like a poor sport.

Lose gracefully. Give the winners a sincere compliment and move on with your life—you have many victories ahead!

Win Like a Boy (Sort Of)

Have you ever listened to a guy tell a story about how he scored the winning goal in his basketball game, or how he picked up a "really hot girl" in the mall? Guys love to win, and when they do, they talk about it. Girls, on the other hand, tend to downplay their successes and play up their failures.

Take a lesson from guys and learn how to accept your victories. Be happy when you win. While you don't want to brag or rub your win in the faces of those who lost, it's okay to be excited and proud about getting something you have worked for. When you get a good grade on a test, do well in sports, or receive an award, give yourself a pat on the back. Be thankful for your win, and don't hide it from others. You've done a great job and deserve congratulations.

So Many Boys, So Little Time

Last month you liked Ethan, but then you met Nate and liked him until two weeks ago when you found out Kyle liked you. You and Kyle are kind of together now, but the more you know him, the less you like him, and now you're interested in Paul. There are so many guys, and you're finding it hard to choose one.

Now is the time to get out and meet those guys! It's perfectly okay to change your mind about guys as you get to know them. A "nice" guy might turn out to be a total jerk, or the "quiet" guy might be the one who wins your heart.

The best way to avoid trouble when dating guys is to be honest. Don't lead a guy along if you know you don't want to get seriously involved. Always let him know that you aren't looking for a serious relationship, and that you want to take time to get to know each other and have fun. Feel free to change your mind and get to know as many guys as you like, but don't play games with their hearts. Keep their feelings in mind as well as your own.

Building a Relationship Takes Two

My parents divorced when I was very young. I saw my dad a lot when I was a child, but our time together slowly dwindled as I got older. When I was fourteen, I hadn't seen my father in two years. I decided I wanted to build on the relationship we had once shared, so I invited him to dinner. However, when we met it was awkward. I had grown up so much in the two years, and he felt like a stranger. I went home immediately after dinner and haven't seen him since.

Not all relationships work out as planned. I would have loved to share a strong bond with my father, but he didn't care about my life at all. No matter how much effort you put in, or how much you care about someone, you must remember that it takes two to make a relationship work. When you have done all you can, accept it, and then move on. If someone isn't willing to accept your love, it is their loss, and there is nothing you can do about it.

The Wheels on the Bus

So you don't have a car and are sick of having your parents chauffeur you around. You need more freedom to go to the public library after school, to your friend's house, to the mall. You want to go according to your schedule, not just when you parents are willing to take you.

Have you ever thought about riding the city bus? Public transportation runs all over the country, and a bus is almost always available to take you where you want to go. When I rode the bus with my friends, we used to enjoy watching the other passengers as we went to the movies: there was the lady who wore headphones and sang along out loud for the whole bus to hear, and the guy with long brown curly hair that puffed out from under his green wool cap. Get a schedule and check out the bus, because you don't need a car to have the freedom of wheels.

Complain, Complain, Complain

We are often told not to complain, to have a good attitude, to smile, and to take bad things in stride instead of getting all worked up. This is good advice, but complaining is not always bad; sometimes it's even healthy. Voicing your opinion can make you feel better about the things you don't like and will help you think of ways to change what angers you.

Make today your day to complain. Whine, cry, and moan about anything and everything that is bothering you. Tell the school principal what really irritates you about school, or write a letter to the editor of your local newspaper and complain about something that happened in your town. Whine about your family to your friends, and about your friends to your family. Complain about everything that has ever gone wrong in your life, and write in your journal all your gripes about the world.

There's always something to complain about, so today, get everything off your chest. Voice your objections and think of ways to change whatever upsets you.

Stuck between a Rock and a Hard Place

It was my sophomore year in high school, and my friend and I both had a crush on the same senior guy. So when he asked me to the prom, I was torn. I wanted to go, but if I said yes, my friend would feel angry and jealous. If I said no, my friend's feelings wouldn't be hurt, but I would possibly pass up the chance for a relationship with a great guy. Either way, I lost.

You will be faced with lose-lose decisions many times during your life. Most choices in life are not black and white, and sometimes you'll have to choose between the lesser of two evils. When you find yourself in a gray area, weigh your options, get advice from people you trust, and go with your heart. Just remember that you won't always find a perfect solution, and that you may be forced to lose something.

For my prom dilemma, I listened to my heart and accepted the invitation. Although my friend was hurt at first, she understood that it was a hard decision for me to make and wasn't mad at me for long. Things tend to work out well in the end.

In April...

Take a nature walk to celebrate the beginning of spring.

Be picture-happy! Start bringing your camera along when you are hanging out with your friends, and take photos of whatever you are doing, even if it's just sitting around.

Put away your winter clothes, and welcome the new season by buying yourself a new shirt or skirt.

Whether bright or soft, wear spring colors at least once a week.

April Fool

"Nobody likes me." "I'm not smart." "There's something wrong with me because I don't have a boyfriend." "I'm such a loser." "I have absolutely no talents."

We girls can be so gullible. If somebody told you that the Earth was flat or that pigs had suddenly started growing wings and could fly, would you believe them? Of course not! The lies we trick ourselves into believing are just as ridiculous, yet we continually convince ourselves that they're true. It's like looking into a funhouse mirror—your face, body, height, and weight are all warped, and you look nothing like yourself. By telling yourself that you are ugly, untalented, stupid, and unpopular, you create a self-image that is nothing like you.

It's time to start seeing a clear picture of yourself. Stop tricking yourself into believing you are less than you really are. Every time you begin to think something negative about yourself, give yourself a compliment and focus on your good qualities. Start seeing yourself with clarity and noticing the brilliant, gorgeous, fun, gifted, amazing girl that you truly are.

A Family of Friends

My friend never invited anyone over to her house, and for the longest time I wondered why. "What is she hiding?" her other friends would wonder. Soon we learned that she was hiding an alcoholic father. She was embarrassed to bring us to her house, and she hated being home herself because she never knew what her father's behavior would be like. She avoided going home at all costs and began hanging out at my house a lot, even when I wasn't there. My house became her home away from home.

If you have problems at home that keep you away, don't feel bad about "adopting" another family, or turning to a friend's parents, an aunt, or a neighbor for the support your own family can't provide. If you have a friend who has problems at home, invite her to be a part of your family. Ask her over for dinner, take her to the movies with your family, let her know that she is always welcome to stay with you whenever she needs to. The wonderful thing about families is that they don't just consist of blood relatives but can extend to whomever we choose to invite in.

Will This Matter When I'm Eighty?

Life as a teenage girl today can be very stressful. You worry about getting good grades, about getting a date for the upcoming dance, and about what other people think of you. Have you ever considered how important these things are in the big picture of your life? When I feel myself worrying about something, I stop and ask myself, "Will this matter to me when I'm eighty?" I usually find that the answer is no.

What kinds of things *will* you remember when you are eighty? You will remember the friendships you made, the love you experienced, the good books you read, the delicious food you ate, the adventures you had, and the artwork you saw. Most likely, you will have forgotten if you got an A or a B on your biology final, or if you were voted "most popular." Today, focus on the things that are most important—the things that touch your heart. They will remain with you for a lifetime.

I Want Him to Call

You've got a new crush. The two of you sit next to each other in math class, you see each other at breaks, and you sometimes sit at the same table for lunch. You like him a lot, and you think he's got feelings for you too, but your relationship hasn't moved past a school friendship. Sitting in your room at night, you dream about him calling you. But he hasn't called, and it's driving you crazy.

It's time to take matters into your own hands and call him! The thought of calling your crush probably makes your nerves go wild, but what have you got to lose? Absolutely nothing! You don't have to have an earth-shattering reason to call, just say hi. Maybe he's shy and just needs a little encouragement from you.

A short telephone conversation might be all you need to learn how much you two have in common, or else it might show you he isn't your type, after all. Either way, you win.

You Are Not a Label

In junior high and high school, it seems that your private business always becomes public knowledge. In an everyone-knows-all environment, people tend to forget our shining moments and dwell on our awful ones instead. The mistakes we've made, things we shouldn't have said, and events we wish we could erase from our past become the markers for how others view us. They become part of who we are—"Sara is the girl who was drunk at the dance and got suspended," or, "Kandra is the girl who got pregnant at fifteen."

Is it any wonder we girls have such a hard time building our self-esteem when everyone is always reminding us of our mess-ups? In the close quarters of school, it is nearly impossible to shake the images people have of you. Today, don't be defined by people's negative labels—remember that these labels are not who *you* are.

What Makes You Happy?

King Midas believed that money was the main ingredient for a happy life. When he was granted one wish, he immediately wished that everything he touched would turn to gold. For awhile Midas enjoyed his golden touch, growing richer as he touched the leaves of a tree or a rock on the ground. When he couldn't eat because his food turned to gold when he touched it, Midas realized that gold didn't always bring happiness.

We all look for happiness in the strangest places. We believe that if we have tons of cute clothes, date a hot guy, or have a "perfect" body, we will be happy. Yet we've got it all wrong. It is not these external things that make us happy, it is the love we receive from our family and the bonds we share with true friends.

Today, pay attention to the people around you. Who is genuinely happy? I bet it isn't always the person with the most money or the best clothes. When do you feel the most happy? When you follow your heart and are with people who you care about, you will discover that then you are happiest with your life.

Appreciating Your Overprotective Parents

One of the most annoying things about being a teen is having parents who constantly have to know whom you are talking to on the phone, whom you are going to be at the movies with, or what time you will be home.

Margaret Mead once said, "One of the oldest human needs is having someone to wonder where you are when you don't come home at night." When I went to college, I realized how true this really is. Because I was living in a dorm without a curfew or someone to answer to, I could come and go as I pleased and stay out as late as I wanted. If I were abducted or hurt, my dorm mates probably wouldn't start to worry until after a few days of not seeing me.

Having someone who worries about you means having someone who loves you. Nobody worries about someone they could care less about. When you are annoyed with your parents and their constant worrying, be patient, and remember that it is a wonderful thing to have people who care.

Dress for Success

Some people say it is shallow to worry about clothes. Not me. Every day I spend at least half an hour deciding what I'm going to wear. I sort through my closet and lay out pairs of jeans, tee shirts, sweaters, and blouses so I can try on different combinations. "How am I feeling today?" I ask myself. "Sassy or sporty?" Whatever the outfit may be, there is always one rule: my clothing must reflect my mood and the way that I am feeling about myself. If I am uncomfortable in my clothing, I feel uncomfortable all day long.

There is nothing wrong with putting effort into your outfits. Take time in the morning or at night before you go to bed to think about how you are feeling and what clothes will make you feel the most confident during the day. What events are planned for the day ahead? Dress in clothes that will fit your activities. Most important, dress the way that makes you feel wonderful, cute, relaxed, and fun. When you are comfortable and confident in your clothes, it will show through in everything you do.

Heavy Hearts

Have you ever felt like you were drowning in sadness? You don't want to get out of bed in the morning, your body is drained of energy, you don't feel like smiling, and you are constantly on the verge of tears. Sadness can be as suffocating as a heavy wool blanket on a hot summer day. It can leave you wondering, "Will I ever feel happy again?"

All I can do is reassure you that everything will get better. I have experienced sadness enough times to know that emotions come and go like the seasons. Just as you know that spring will come after a long winter, you should trust that happiness will fill your heart again soon.

When you are sad, draw on your inner courage, have faith, and always remember that even the hardest times will eventually pass.

Take a Risk

Today is your day to take a risk and do something that makes you nervous. Challenge makes life exciting, and facing your fears will strengthen your spirit. Run for student body office or the cheer squad. Volunteer to give a speech at the upcoming assembly, or try out for the lead role in the school play. You will be proud of yourself when you succeed.

"What if I don't succeed," you ask? You may fail, but not always. Everyone fails sometimes; that's part of being human. The way you deal with your failure shows your character. Learn from your failure by asking yourself, "What could I have done better?" Then move on. People won't think of you as a loser, and chances are they will forget about your failure more quickly than you will. When you don't win, it means that there is something better for you out there—so go find it!!

Find a way to challenge yourself, and don't let fear of failure get in your way. If you don't try something, you won't win anything.

Don't Take Mean Things to Heart

When I was fourteen, a guy said I had flabby arms and nicknamed me "Chicken Wings." That got me worrying about my arms, and now, six years later, I'm still self-conscious. I look at pictures of myself wearing short-sleeved shirts and say, "Yuck! Look at how big and ugly my arms are!"

It's amazing how one little thing said during your teens can stick with you for your entire life. When people make fun of you, it's usually because of their own insecurities. Maybe they're jealous of you and are trying to feel better about themselves by making fun of you. Maybe they want attention from you and don't know how to get it other than by teasing.

I recently talked to the guy who called me Chicken Wings and told him how self-conscious his comments made me. He said, "I can't believe that upset you so much because I was totally kidding!" Keep this in mind, and try not to take to heart the mean things that people say to you.

I Don't Want to Grow Up

You are eager to grow up, to be older and independent. You count the days until you can get your driver's license and freedom, you dream of the day you won't have to ask your parents' permission to go places, and you think about getting extra money by working.

It *is* wonderful to grow up and experience new things. In spite of all the wonderful gains that age brings, with every rite of passage and piece of life knowledge you gain, a part of your innocence is gone forever. With the excitement of growing up, you may not even notice the losses. One day, you will feel nostalgic and say, "I remember how fun it was in junior high when my mom would drive us to the school dances," or, "My summers were so relaxing before I had to get a job."

Today, focus on how wonderful it is to be young. Be open to the excitement that youth offers you. Don't be in a hurry to grow up, or get anxious about learning how to drive, or wish that you had already graduated from high school. Enjoy your youth because it will be over sooner than you think.

I'm Gonna Have to Say No

It's Friday night, and even though you've planned to relax at home, when your friend asks you to go to a party with her, you say yes. Or your parents are gone and you're at home watching a movie with a guy you really like. You kiss, and then he starts moving too fast, but instead of stopping him, you continue.

If you find that these types of situations are occurring in your life, it's time to learn the power of the little word *no*. Saying no can be hard because you worry that you will disappoint people, or that they will dislike you. What you may fail to realize is that by always saying yes, you could be hurting yourself.

Today, practice saying no. Whatever the situation is, don't say yes unless it is something you really want to do. There's no need to give an excuse for why you are saying no; it is often best to simply say, "No. I'm sorry, I can't do that." Learning to say no takes practice and courage because it means turning another person down in order to put yourself first. Just remember, you can do it.

It's Okay to Say No to Me

You didn't do your science homework because you spent the whole night talking on the phone and watching MTV. You beg your best friend to let you copy her assignment before class, but she says no. You are furious, not at yourself for slacking off, but at your friend. How could she say no to you?

Before you fly off the handle, remember that both you and your friends should be able to say no when you need to. It's important to learn how to deal with being turned down because it will happen many times in your life. Let your friends know that it is okay to say no to you. Don't badger a friend who says she doesn't want to go to the party on Saturday night, or refuse to speak to a friend who refuses to let you borrow her black sweater. Show people that you will not pout or get angry, but that you will still be their friend if they turn you down. If you encourage others to say no when they need to, they will respect you when you feel the need to do the same.

Will You Come to the Bathroom with Me?

"Why do girls go everywhere in big groups?" Ryan asked me.

"We don't!" I said defensively.

"Yes, you do! Girls are always going to the bathroom together, or walking down the halls in big clans. It's so annoying how you always have to be together!"

Girls do tend to travel in packs. We continually go to lunch together, parties together, the mall together, or class together. We go together to buy soda at halftime of the basketball game, and to call our moms to tell them we'll be home soon.

Today, travel alone. Don't insist that your friends come to the bathroom, down the hall, and everywhere else with you. While it is fun to have company, there is something you're missing out on if you're always tied to a buddy— freedom. I used to insist on driving myself to parties because it meant that I could leave whenever I wanted. When you go places by yourself, you have the freedom to move at your own pace without being rushed or waiting for your slowpoke friend, and you can stop and talk to whomever you pass.

I've Got Work to Do, but All I Can Think about Is a Khaki Skirt

Have you ever been studying for a test or writing a paper when your mind starts wandering? You think about the movie you watched last night, the cute khaki skirt you saw at the mall, or your plans for Friday night—everything except your homework. Isn't it funny how our minds can wander at the most inopportune times?

Learning to discipline yourself is difficult, and for some of us it seems next to impossible. I've often used bribery to keep my mind on track. I promise myself that I will go buy that cute khaki skirt if I get a certain amount of work done in a certain amount of time. If I don't finish my work, I don't get the skirt.

If you are having trouble with self-discipline, try the bribery technique. Tell yourself that if you get your paper finished two days before it is due, you will give yourself a free day with no worries, or you will buy some scented bath soaps and give yourself a spa night. A little incentive may be all you need to get your mind on the right track.

Ignore Others' Cruelty

During my sophomore year in high school, a group of senior girls made it their mission to make my best friend's life miserable. They didn't like her, and they let her know this by glaring at her when she walked down the halls, calling her a slut and starting vicious rumors about her, "decorating" her house with toilet paper, and egging her car.

If you're the target of vicious harassment, the best strategy is to just ignore it. Try to remain calm and collected. If you cry, yell, or get worked up, you will give them the reaction they want. Hold your head high and walk by without saying a word or looking in their direction. When you see one of them and are feeling courageous, look them in the eye, smile, and say, "How are you doing today?" This will show them you are above their cruel tactics and that their immaturity is not affecting your happiness.

If the harassment continues and you worry for your safety, don't hesitate to get help. Talk to your parents, a teacher, or school counselor. Most important, remember that when people are mean to you, it's a sign of their immaturity.

Listen to Me

Being a good listener is much harder than many people think. Listening is not just about hearing what another person says. Good listening means letting another person talk and giving them your full attention without interrupting them. It means thinking about the meaning behind what someone is saying.

It's important to have someone in your life who is a good listener, someone whom you can talk to about your dreams and worries without feeling like you have to fight to get a word in. Someone who listens to you without giving you advice on what they would do in your situation.

Don't waste your time telling your important thoughts to someone who is always talking about themselves. Those kind of people may hear what you said, but they don't really listen. Good listeners are hard to find, but they are worth their weight in gold. Make it a point to practice *your* good listening skills, too.

Be Responsible...

Responsibility! It's the characteristic that goes hand in hand with growing older. The first time your mother lets you stay at home by yourself, she asks, "Can I trust you to be responsible?" Your teachers tell you it is your responsibility to pay attention in class and turn your homework in on time. When you have a job, you must show up to work on time, get your job done, and budget your money—all three things done responsibly, of course.

Being a responsible person means getting chores and studies, all your "have-to's" done on time. It means promptly returning something you borrowed from a friend. When you are responsible, people will trust you, ask you for help, give you freedom, and look up to you as a leader. Knowing that people count on you to act responsibly, and to do what you say you'll do, is a wonderful feeling. Today, take on some responsibility, and prove your capability to be responsible.

. . .But Don't Forget to Be Fun

Remember when you were in elementary school and your teacher always picked a kid to watch the room when she was gone? The kid she picked was responsible for making sure nobody did anything wrong. Most likely, she picked him because he took life so seriously and never had much fun—he was always being so darn responsible.

Responsibility can have many rewards, but it also can be quite a drag. Think of the friend you have nicknamed "Mom" because she's always saying, "We shouldn't do that. It's not the *right* thing to do." Don't make your life dull by becoming so responsible that you are no longer playful.

Responsibility means having the ability to respond. It does not mean always being dull and adultlike; having fun is not a bad thing. Being responsible means learning when to respond in seriousness and when to respond in playfulness. Today, mix responsibility with fun, and find a balance that works for you.

Act Like Yourself

In junior high and high school, I wanted to be popular so badly that I lost myself. Everything I did—the people I talked to, the clothes I wore, and the things I said—were all done to get people to like me. I worried that if I spent too much time talking to the "nerds" I would never be cool, so I focused on getting the attention of the "popular" people. I wasn't a snob, I was just scared of being rejected, of being without friends, and of being labeled a "dork."

I finally figured out that depending on others' acceptance to define your self-worth will only leave you feeling unfulfilled. When you make popularity your main goal, you constantly change your personality to fit those around you. As Bonnie M. Parsley says in her book *The Choice Is Yours*, "When we make belonging a need, we cannot feel free to be ourselves." Instead of acting like yourself, you constantly say and do things to give others a particular image of you.

Today, put aside your desire for popularity, and focus on just being yourself.

Healthy Relationships

When I was asked as a teen to describe my perfect guy, I would invent a guy who possessed the best qualities from past boyfriends, guys I had crushes on, and my best guy friends. "My ideal guy," I would respond, "would have Scott's sense of humor, Ryan's intelligence, Brent's athletic abilities, and be caring and thoughtful like Nick."

Today, think about what qualities your perfect guy would have, as well as what makes a healthy relationship. Many girls think that a healthy relationship means a long-term relationship, but that isn't always true. Having a variety of guys in your life instead of one long-term boyfriend helps you discover which qualities you find most important in a boyfriend. Remember, you can learn a lot about dating and relationships from all the guys around you, whether he's your boyfriend, just a boy friend, a boy you dated once, or someone in between.

I'm Going Out-Without My Boy

In junior high and high school, I had a friend who always had a boyfriend; she'd break up with one boyfriend and start dating a new guy the next week. I had another friend who spent all of her free time with her boyfriend.

One of the most important aspects of a healthy relationship is spending time away from the relationship. Tell your boyfriend you're going to spend the weekend with your girlfriends, give yourself time to be single in between boyfriends, or simply soak in the tub alone instead of talking to him on the phone. Time apart is as equally important to a relationship as time together, and it gives you both the chance to unwind, reflect, think, and see your relationship clearly. When you are away from your boyfriend, you appreciate and enjoy your time together much more than when you spend every waking hour with him.

When you have a boyfriend, don't ditch your friends, stop having alone time, or cut back on doing the things you enjoy. Encourage him to spend time without you, too. You will find that as two individuals, each with your own lives, you will make a stronger, happier couple.

First Things First

Which comes first in a relationship, a friendship or physical attraction? This question isn't as simple as it sounds. You have be physically attracted to a guy in order to get into a relationship with him, but it's also important to keep the physical side of your relationship from getting too far ahead of friendship. Often we follow our hormones first—hooking up with a crush at a party, or kissing a guy before the two of you have had a real conversation, hoping that a relationship will grow from that one kiss.

Most healthy relationships don't start from a hookup. In order to grow properly, a relationship needs a stronger foundation than just physical attraction. If there is a guy you really like, get to know him as a friend, find out his interests, and see what you have in common. The physical side of the relationship should come after you've discovered there is a stronger connection than just physical attraction.

Boyfriend Blind Spots

Love is blind; it allows you to care about another person regardless of his or her imperfections. This same blindness that lets us love unconditionally can also make us oblivious to major problems in those we love.

There are some mistakes you shouldn't forgive a guy for, like cheating on you, lying to you, drinking excessively, hitting you, putting you down, or losing his temper. Often we girls are willing to sacrifice our own well-being just so we can stay in a relationship. We make excuses for our boyfriend's misbehavior and continually forgive him for repeated offenses. Sure, everyone makes mistakes and deserves a second chance, but not a third, fourth, and fifth chance.

Today, be aware of your boyfriend blind spots. See your relationship for what it is truly like, not for what you wish it were like, or for what it could be like if only your boyfriend would change. You deserve to be treated like a princess, and if you stand up for yourself, one day you'll find your prince.

Counting on Him to Make You Happy

It was my birthday, and everyone was celebrating but me. My friends had put up signs that read "It's Amanda's Birthday" all around school, and they had also brought me flowers and balloons. Everywhere I went, people were wishing me a happy birthday. Even with all the recognition, I still wasn't happy. Shawn, the guy I had a crush on and had been "kinda talking to," never wished me a happy birthday. Instead of rejoicing in all the love I was receiving, I felt like my birthday was completely ruined because this one person didn't say, "Happy birthday."

Have you ever let a boy decide how your day will go? You have a wonderful day if he says hi to you in the halls or asks you have lunch with him, but if he passes you without a word or sits with another girl at lunch, your entire day is ruined.

Whether he's your boyfriend or a guy you are just getting to know, you can't base all of your happiness on his actions. Today, remember that you can have a good day *regardless* of how he is acting.

Not Romeo and Juliet

Romeo and Juliet are probably the greatest lovers in history. Many people find it romantic that Romeo and Juliet kill themselves in the end because they can't live without each other. I think it's a sign of an unhealthy relationship. Just think, if Romeo hadn't been so impulsive, he would have been overwhelmed with joy when he found that Juliet was only faking death. If Romeo could have been able to live without Juliet, the two may have been happily together forever.

Many girls think that if they suffer a lot and are miserable when they are away from their boyfriends, it shows how much they love them. Misery is a sign of dependency, not love. Statements like, "I couldn't live without you," or, "I'd kill myself if I didn't have you," do not equal love.

You should be able to live without your boyfriend, and he should be able to live without you. This doesn't mean that you aren't in love; it just shows that you both have a healthy outlook on your relationship.

He Should Return Your Love

I once had a boyfriend who didn't return my shows of affection. To let him know that I cared, I would make him cards, bake him cookies, call just to say hi, give him good luck charms before baseball games, and help him with his homework. He never did much for me in return. I would tell myself, "I'm doing these things because I love him, not because I am hoping for something in return," but I secretly wished he would do something to show me that he cared.

A relationship is give and take, not something where you're doing all the giving. It is important that your boyfriend returns your acts of love. It doesn't matter what he does—whether he writes you a poem, brings you flowers, asks you how your day is going, or helps you practice for volleyball tryouts—as long as he shows he cares for you.

If a guy truly cares for you, he will tell you, but more important, he will also show you. If you're doing all the work in the relationship, it may be time to think about what's really going on.

Playing the Game

At the start of a relationship, there is always a game going on. We are afraid of being vulnerable, so we hide many of our true feelings by playing hard to get, not calling, or flat-out refusing to say, "I like you."

There is a point when relationship games can be taken too far, however. A guy has crossed the line if he only shows you he likes you some of the time; tells you that you're his girlfriend, but then tells his friends that you aren't; or strings along several girls at one time. A guy who plays games is dishonest and won't be the kind of boyfriend you deserve.

Remember, games can go both ways, so don't play around with guys' hearts, and don't put up with guys who play with yours. You will be happier in your relationships if both of you are honest with each other.

Battling Big Group Phobia

Do you ever feel alone even when you're around tons of friends? Sometimes I feel the most lonely when I'm in a big group of people, because instead of just enjoying the people I'm with, I start comparing myself to others. I worry, thinking to myself, "No guys want to talk to me because I'm not as cute as she is," or, "If only I were funnier, people would be excited I'm here."

Big group gatherings can be difficult if you are a one-on-one type of person. Next time you go to a party, get a more outgoing friend to help you out. Let her know that group settings make you nervous, and ask her to introduce you to people you don't know and to include you in conversations. Then take a deep breath, relax, and just be yourself.

In May. . .

Surprise your mother with a special treat when she's least expecting it.

Go to the library and check out A. A. Milne's Complete Works of Winnie the Pooh. *Read a different story every night. You'll be surprised how much you can learn from that little yellow bear.*

Get a bouquet of fresh flowers for your room.

Flowers for May Day

May has arrived, and what better way to greet its debut than with a May Day celebration? For centuries, people worldwide have honored May 1 as a symbol of the rebirth of nature and the liveliness of human spirit. The Romans would collect flowers and tree branches early in the morning and, after crowning a May Day queen, they would dance and sing all day long. The French say that wearing lilies-of-the-valley on May 1 will bring good luck; any wish you make while wearing them will come true. During my childhood, my friends and I used to pick flowers and secretly leave them on the doorsteps of our neighbors with a "Happy May Day" note.

Celebrate May Day by delivering flowers to your family, friends, neighbors, and teachers—even to strangers. Get a vase of fresh flowers for yourself, wear a floral dress, make a daisy chain, and put flowers in your hair. You will feel the spirit of spring with all these flowers around you.

Dancing Queen

Feeling sad, low-energy, and bored? Feeling excited, pumped-up, and ready to go? The perfect thing for any mood is a dance party! I'm talking go crazy, cut-a-rug type dancing. My friends and I used to create our own private dance club in my room by sliding all my bedroom furniture against the walls and putting on our favorite dance-mix tape. I still love to have dance parties in my room; my college roommate nicknamed me "Dancing Queen" because I'm always dancing around our room.

There is something almost magical about dancing. When you turn up the music and start moving, you lose all your worries, and a smile you just can't seem to wipe away appears on your face. Dancing makes you feel alive and excited. The best thing about dance parties is that they can happen any time and any place—by yourself, with a few friends, or with fifty classmates.

Be a dancing queen and throw a dance party. I guarantee you'll love it!

Help Someone Feel Included

Have you ever had to eat lunch by yourself, been in a class where you don't know a single person, or changed schools so you were the "new kid"? We all know the loneliness of feeling like an outsider. Think about how good it would have felt if, during your lonely times, someone had started a conversation with you, invited you to eat lunch with her friends, or simply said hello.

Many girls are so busy putting all of their effort into making sure they aren't alone that they don't ever notice other people's loneliness. Today, look around you and notice one person who is isolated or cut off from others. Maybe it's a friend, an acquaintance, or even someone you don't know at all. Make an effort to smile, say hello, ask how they are doing, and introduce yourself. Who knows, you may even make a new friend.

Dealing with Mom

Getting along with your mother can seem nearly impossible at times. She makes ridiculous rules and asks stupid questions. She nags you about your homework or putting away the dishes. She won't let you talk on the phone past nine o'clock, borrow the car Friday night, or stay out all night after the school dance. Your mother can drive you absolutely crazy! The two of you probably argue about anything, and sometimes you dream of the day you can move away from her.

Every day, our mothers continue to do so much for us, even when we are acting far from nice. There are probably many things your mother does that go unnoticed, like packing your lunch, driving you to the mall to meet your friends, helping you apply for a job, or folding your laundry.

With Mother's Day around the corner, remember all the wonderful things your mother does for you. Nobody is perfect; neither is your mother. This Mother's Day, let your mom know how much you care about her. Make her a card titled "Fifty Things I Love about My Mother," or tell her how much you appreciate her hard work.

Loving Your Body

When the weather warms up, winter clothes are traded for tank tops and shorts, and one worry enters just about every teenage girl's mind: "What will I look like in my swimsuit?" You become consumed with all your body's faults, criticizing your flabby thighs, round tummy, or small boobs. You swear to go on a strict diet and lose ten pounds by June. You promise yourself, "I can do it if I eat only salad with no dressing and work out everyday."

Stop right there! Stop obsessing about the way you could look if you were a computerized and plastic-surgery-enhanced model. Start loving your body the way it is. It sounds cheesy and unrealistic, but it *is* possible. Learn to feel good about your body, faults and all, or you're going to be miserable.

Today, after you get out of the shower or before you go to bed, look at yourself in a mirror. Wear your bra and underwear, a swimsuit, or be naked—however you feel comfortable—just do it! Find a part of your body you think looks pretty good, one that other girls envy. Say, "I have great (body part)!" Your thoughts will create your reality.

Fishing for Compliments

"I'm so fat!" I say loudly enough for every girl at the table to hear. They look at me in shock.

"You are not fat, Amanda," one girl responds.

"I am fat!" I reply. "I have elephant thighs."

"At least your skin isn't as white as a ghost's," another replies.

We've all been a part of it. You and your girlfriends sitting around complaining about your bodies, your faces, or your hair. You're really just fishing for compliments. By saying, "I am so ugly," you hope to have someone reply, "No you aren't. You're beautiful." Your fears are momentarily put to rest because now someone has assured you that you aren't ugly.

Today, don't participate in self-bashing for the sake of earning compliments, and keep quiet when others start complaining about themselves. Think of the positive aspects of your body (remember yesterday?) — you don't have to say them out loud, just think them to yourself. Tearing yourself down so that others can bring you up will not build your positive self-image. While others point out their body flaws, focus on your great legs, clear complexion, and cute nose.

Skinny or Healthy?

I once had a friend with an eating disorder. She would have an apple and a Diet Coke for lunch and then go for a run after school. Looking at her face and body, you could see how unhealthy she was, but as she lost more and more weight, girls would say, "I wish I had her will power so I wouldn't eat so much."

It's terrible what we put ourselves through just to be skinny. We will do anything to be thin, even if it means ruining our bodies. Some girls think that being healthy means eating only fruits and vegetables, but that will not give you all the nutrients that your body needs to survive.

Today, start examining your relationship with food. What have you eaten today? Do you feel guilty when you eat something "bad" for you? Pay attention because your body will tell you when you're being unhealthy. Eating healthy should come from your desire to be good to your body, not your desire to be skinny.

If Only I Looked Like She Does

"I'm so ugly!" I'd think to myself. "If only I looked like she does, my life would be better. Boys would like me, I'd have more friends, teachers would give me better grades, and I'd have nothing to worry about."

We girls have an amazing ability to see beauty, but only in others. We look at girls around us and find wonderful qualities—her eyes are bright blue or she has a clear complexion—but we always see ourselves as ugly, fat, and less attractive than everyone around us.

Comparing yourself to other girls is pointless. You'll never look like someone else. The face and body you see in the mirror every day are the ones you'll have for the rest of your life, so you might as well start appreciating your looks right now. Stop thinking that the grass is always greener on the other side of the fence. "Pretty" girls wish they looked different, too.

Today, stop yourself when you begin to think, "Why can't my nose look like hers?" Instead of putting your energy into wishing you looked liked some other girl, put your energy into bringing out your own beautiful qualities. Name three of them right now.

Love Those Workouts

What comes into mind when you think of working out? Do you imagine painful hours of lifting weights and walking endlessly on a stair climber, or do you hear the voice of a perky aerobics instructor telling you to keep going even though you're about to drop? It's no wonder so many girls hate working out—for them, it's *work*.

Exercise is important for both your physical and your mental health. It keeps your heart and lungs strong, it raises your energy level, and it helps increase your self-esteem. To make exercise work for you, your workouts need to be fun. If you're doing something that is hard and boring, you probably won't want to keep exercising.

Today, exercise in a way you enjoy. Swim, play tennis, ride a bike, walk in the park, or join a sports team; when the sun is shining, the options for fun exercise are endless. Rollerblading is my favorite workout. I love it, and I skate for hours without even realizing that I'm working. When you have fun, you won't have to force yourself to exercise because it will be something you look forward to doing.

Too Much Exercise

Although exercise is great for your body, too much of it can hurt you. It may sound ridiculous, but many girls become addicted to exercising. They push their bodies too far by going for a run, lifting weights, and doing aerobics all in one day. Some even continue to exercise when they are tired, sick, or have injuries.

Even though your body needs exercise, it also needs rest. Listen to your body, and don't push yourself beyond what you can do. If you are tired, short of breath, or feel dizzy or nauseated, it's time to stop. Keep in mind that a healthy amount of exercise is about an hour a day.

Overexercising won't give you healthy results sooner; it will only hurt you. You will have more energy and get more out of your exercise when you give your body time to rest.

Need Help Boosting Your Body Image?

Loving your body is not as easy as simply saying, "I'm going to start being happy with the way I look." We are indirectly taught that looks are the measure of a girl's value, so we feel our bodies are never quite right. When you have a poor body image, your self-esteem can take a huge dive, making you feel terrible about every aspect of your life.

If you can't boost your body image on your own, it's time to get some help. Talk to a school counselor, a leader at your church, a doctor, or anyone with whom you feel comfortable discussing your body image. Don't feel embarrassed to ask for help; you may find that talking with someone helps you better understand your feelings and allows you to come up with solutions you wouldn't have thought of on your own.

Creating a positive body image can take years, and for some women it is a lifetime struggle. So get help and start loving your body today. The sooner you do, the happier you will become with all parts of your self.

Give a Compliment

"Have I ever told you my pretty feet story?" my mom asks.

"No," I lie. I've heard the story so many times that I know it by heart, but I can sense she wants to tell it again, so I humor her.

"I was trying on a pair of shoes, and the salesman said to me, 'You have very pretty feet.' I'd never really thought of myself as having particularly pretty feet, but as I looked down to see what he was talking about, I saw that I did have really pretty feet! It just took someone to point it out to me, I guess."

We all have pretty parts of our bodies, but it's hard for us to see them for ourselves. Sometimes all we need is one small compliment to make us aware of our own beauty.

Today, help boost other girls' self-images. Give them compliments about their bodies, their hair, their faces. Point out something particularly beautiful about them. One small compliment from you may change a person's life. I'll bet that salesman had no clue what a lasting impact he'd have on my mother the day he pointed out her pretty feet.

If All Else Fails, Pray

I had been in a slump for weeks, emotionally and physically. My mother and I had been arguing, my friends seemed to be ignoring me, and I had been overwhelmed with homework. The science fair was coming up in a week, too, and I didn't think I was going to survive long enough to get all the research finished. I cried every day, I was always tired, and I constantly wondered when life would be fun again. I had come to the end of my rope.

Sometimes, when life is bad, it just keeps getting worse. We try everything we can think of to make things better, but we can't seem to get back on the right track. That's when I pray. As poet Alfred, Lord Tennyson said, "More things are wrought by prayer than this world dreams of."

Prayers can solve life's problems, although we don't always see the outcome right away. Believe me, though, there is immense power in prayer. When all else fails, pray for the calmness and strength to get through tough times.

Let's Make a Deal

Here's a plan to help you strike just about any deal with your parents. Whenever you want something from them, like money for a new pair of jeans, a later curfew, a tattoo, or an end to the piano lessons your mother insists on, approach your parents calmly.

Have your arguments mapped out. Simply saying "I really want to do this" isn't going to win your parents over. Explain why you want what you want and why it isn't a frivolous request.

After you have spoken, listen quietly to your parents' questions and concerns. Don't get mad when they say something you don't like. Stay calm and listen carefully to their feelings. Be flexible and willing to meet your parents halfway. A compromise is better than nothing.

Once you have come to a compromise, stick with it. You absolutely must do what you and your parents have agreed upon, even if you have to sacrifice part of what you wanted to reach this compromise. If you break your word, you will lose your parents' trust, and the next time you have a request, your parents won't be open to listening.

Why Do People Think I'm a Snob?

When I was in junior high and high school, many people thought I was a snob. I wasn't a snob, I was just insecure and afraid of being rejected. I talked a lot when I was with my friends, but when I was around people I didn't know well, I said very little. This quietness led others to believe "She thinks she's better than everyone else."

Sometimes you may feel that people see you as someone completely opposite of who you really are. In an attempt to hide your fears, your insecurities may cause you to act differently—the girl who worries she isn't good enough comes across as conceited, or the one who feels ugly actually appears vain. Be patient; outgrowing insecurities is an ongoing process. The more you are willing to face your self-doubts, the more comfortable you will become with yourself, and the easier it will be to reveal your *real* self.

I'm Outgrowing My Friends

Outgrowing friends is hard and can leave you feeling lost. Yet it is a natural part of growing up because we don't all grow in the same ways. Maybe you and your best friend played soccer together since the time you were seven, or you became close friends with two girls because your boyfriends were best friends. When your friend quit soccer to run track and you found a new boyfriend, you and your friends slowly drifted apart.

Remember, not all friends are here to stay. People come into our lives because they fit a need for a particular time. When your life changes and you no longer need the same things, you may no longer need the same friendships you once did. You outgrow friends just like you outgrow a pair of jeans or tennis shoes. It's okay to change as you grow up, and it's okay to feel like you need new friends.

Cherish your friendships while you have them, but know when it is time to let them go. Don't worry, new people will come into your life.

Teaching Adults

Many adults have stamped teens with a "bad" label. They say we are lazy, foolish, irrational, untrustworthy, difficult. It's too bad that these adults don't realize that older does not necessarily mean wiser—there is a lot they could learn from us "terrible teens."

Today, teach an adult something. Show your mom how to use a new computer program, tell the principal your solution for a problem that's been going on at school, or invite your neighbor who never seems to smile to the funny school play you're in. Show those adults that teens are passionate, ambitious, energetic, hopeful, intuitive, and smart.

Nike Is a Girl!

For a long, long time, our society has associated sports and competition with men. Only recently have women been allowed to participate seriously in athletics. Our society is lagging behind in this arena, especially considering that in ancient Greece, the goddess in charge of all athletics was a girl.

Nike, which is Greek for "victory," was the goddess of competition; she was the deity male athletes prayed to when playing sports. She inspired them to play hard, helped them to win, and was seen as the holder of ultimate athletic power.

Today, get out there and play sports. Don't listen to guys who say, "Girls can't play football, softball is wimpy, and girls' basketball sucks!" Kick some butt, be a victorious athlete, and remember, Nike is a girl!

The Best Revenge Is a Life Well Lived

Tyler was outgoing and fun to be with. His sense of humor, chivalrous attitude, and athletic talent drew me to him; even though we'd only been together for three months, he was my dream guy. That is, until I found out he cheated on me. When I learned that, I wanted revenge. I thought about dating his best friend to make him jealous, or embarrassing him by telling everyone the private things he had told me.

Even though I wanted to get back at Tyler, I thought of the saying "The best revenge is a life well lived." Instead of letting someone's cruelty bring you down, the best revenge is to make your life better than it was before he came around. Freaking out and trying to make his life terrible will inevitably leave you looking like the fool. You can feel great about yourself when your boyfriend breaks up with you if you show up to school happy and cheerful. When your best friend ditches you for a new group, go out and make new friends who care about you instead of plotting ways to make her miserable. Turn your desire for revenge into motivation to make your life better.

Embrace Diversity

Look around you and notice all the faces you see; no two are exactly alike and each has its own uniqueness. America is full of diversity, and it is important to celebrate all the different groups that have helped to develop our culture.

Chinese, Irish, African American, Native American, Latino, Swedish, or Filipino, our ethnic background is part of who we are and helps shape our life. Today, find out the background of a friend who is a different ethnicity than you are. Where is her family from? What ethnicity does she consider herself? Did her parents immigrate to America, or have they been here for hundreds of years?

Never make an assumption about a person based on the color of his or her skin. Instead, ask questions and have discussions about racial issues with your friends. Remember that racism affects everyone—the more we learn about different races, the more we will embrace diversity and put an end to hate.

Being a Spoiled Brat

Whenever I was being, as my mother put it, "a spoiled brat," she would say to me, "Remember that I owe you only few things in life: a place to live, a few clothes so that you don't go naked, love, and food. Everything else I give you comes from the goodness of my heart." That always frustrated me, but it also left me speechless. It was true. I had a wonderful home with my own bedroom, a closet full of clothes, a kitchen stocked with my favorite foods, and an overabundant supply of love. My mother really didn't *owe* me anything else.

Acting like a spoiled brat means demanding that your family goes out for Mexican food when everyone else feels like burgers, putting a guilt trip on your parents when they won't buy you a new outfit, or demanding that you get a raise in your allowance and then pouting when you don't get your way. Be thankful today for what you do have, because there are many people in the world who don't have nearly as much as you do.

Why Did I Even Bother Curling My Hair?

Glancing sleepily at my clock, I saw that it was 8:30 A.M. I dozed off for a moment before I remembered: "Tonight's the homecoming dance, and Brian will be here in eight hours!!" Thoughts of everything I had to do were rushing through my head: take a shower, get my hair and nails done, pick up the boutonniere. I ran to the mirror and smiled when I saw that no unexpected blemishes had appeared overnight. While waiting for my avocado face mask to dry, I called Brian to see if he was as excited about the night as I was. I got my answer when his mother said, "He's still asleep."

We girls tend to get quite excited over boys, but you may be hurt or disappointed when you realize he isn't as excited about you. Maybe he stood you up. Maybe you didn't get the kiss you hoped for, or he dropped the "Let's just be friends" line. Times like these leave every girl asking, "Why did I even bother curling my hair?"

Placing super-high expectations on a guy sets you up for potential hurt. Try not to read more into a guy's actions than there actually is.

Music to Match Your Many Moods

When my friends flip through my CD collection, they always say, "You have the most random taste in music." From Sarah McLachlan to Led Zeppelin, Madonna to George Strait, Mozart to Puff Daddy, I've got music to fit my every mood.

Music plays a big part in how you feel, so pay close attention to your music selection. Need to relax? Try Enya. Going on a summer afternoon picnic? Bob Marley is always a good choice. Broaden your musical horizons by listen to a new radio station; maybe you'll discover a sound that fits you just right. Music is a powerful tool, so remember, if you want to change your mood, change your music.

It's Always Good
to Be a Food Snob

I love food and always try to eat things that make my taste buds joyful. Today, that means a fresh green salad with Roma tomatoes, onions, avocados, and grilled chicken with balsamic vinaigrette. My friends constantly tease me about the time I brought salmon and potatoes wrapped in tin foil so I could barbecue them at a tail-gate party where everyone else was eating hot dogs and chips. "You're such a food snob," they say. I always reply, "What better thing to be a snob about than food?"

Listen to your body and choose your food carefully. Are you craving a turkey sandwich, a bowl of fruit, a glass of milk, or a hamburger? Don't fight your cravings because they tell you when your body needs certain nutrients. Enjoy what you eat, and savor the flavor and delicious spices. Treat yourself to more than just peanut butter and jelly for lunch, and watch how much more satisfied and happy you will feel. It's okay to be a snob about food.

Every Girl Is in the Same Boat

One night, my girlfriends and I were driving around. Everyone was laughing and singing along to the radio, but I wasn't in the mood. For some reason I felt sad and quiet inside. When one of my girlfriends asked jokingly, "What's wrong with you?" I immediately burst into tears.

"I'm feeling so sad, and I don't know why."

My friend next to me gave me a hug and said, "Do you think I'm happy? I feel sad, too. I'm just pretending to have fun, hoping it will make me feel better."

Hearing my friend say that was a huge revelation for me. I always thought all my friends were better off than I was; they were prettier, smarter, and funnier than I was. I always thought I was the only one who ever felt unhappy or like a failure. That night I learned my friends were hiding their upsets just as I had been.

Every teenage girl is in the same boat—we all feel heartsick at times, depressed for no reason, and lonely even when we're with friends. Even if you and your friends don't talk about it, know that you are not alone in your sadness.

Put an End to Procrastination

One day I sat in my room listening to music, talking on the phone, and watching television. I painted my nails, played solitaire, cleaned my room, arranged my CDs in alphabetical order, and even made a sign for my door that read, "The Palace of Procrastination. Why do today what you can put off until tomorrow?" I found every excuse I could for putting off the homework I knew I'd have to start sooner or later.

As you may have noticed, procrastination is a hard pattern to break. We put off our homework until Sunday night, and put off our workouts until Monday morning. You may have noticed you procrastinate in other areas of your life: you say that you'll forgive your friends once they apologize to you, you'll stop arguing with your parents when they stop being so overprotective, and you'll make a fresh start next year and get all straight A's.

Stop waiting around for outside forces to be the catalyst that gets you moving. Making up your mind to take action is the only thing needed to get things done in your life.

I Want a Boyfriend!

Life wakes in springtime—flowers bloom, trees blossom, and the days become longer. Another thing is rekindled with the arrival of spring—love. Cupid seems to be working overtime when the sun starts to shine. New couples pop up everywhere, strolling hand in hand and sharing parting kisses as they go to class. If you have remained unbitten by the lovebug, you may long to be one of those girls with stars in her eyes and find yourself sighing, "I want a boyfriend."

Stop right there! Life's difficult when you feel like the only girl who's not in a relationship. You wish you had a guy to hold hands with and talk on the phone to. Finding a boyfriend just for the sake of having a guy to call your own, however, goes against the purpose of a relationship. A rewarding relationship only comes when you both *really* like each other and share common interests and experiences together.

You are *not* the only girl without a boyfriend. Everyone is single at one time or another. When the time is right, you will find a boyfriend, and your relationship will be stronger and full of true love because you waited for the right guy.

Left Off the Guest List

"Are you going to Kevin's party, Amanda?"

"No. I don't want to go," I said, but I hadn't even been invited to Kevin's party.

"Why? It is going to be the best party of the year! You can't miss it."

"I don't like Kevin," I said, trying to cover up my hurt feelings, "and I have other, more important, plans."

Being left off a guest list can make you feel completely rejected, especially when all your friends are invited and you aren't. I still remember the night when Kevin, a guy I thought was my friend, threw his party, and I sat at home and cried, imagining all my friends having a blast without me.

If something like this happens to you, just remember, there will be more parties; this party isn't the be all and end all of parties. Don't sit at home feeling miserable and rejected, go out and do something fun for yourself. Invite a friend to go to the movies or to spend the night. Remember, nobody's going to think you're a loser because you weren't invited to this one party; in two weeks, nobody will even remember who was and wasn't there.

I Hate My Siblings!

Have you ever asked yourself, "How could I come from the same family as my siblings?" Your brother is always complaining and hates everything you like; your sister is quiet and completely unathletic; and you are outgoing and live for sports. You are total opposites, and your siblings are not the type of people you'd ever choose as your friends. Unfortunately, you can't pick your family, so you have no control over the fact that you have to associate with your siblings.

Family is a weird thing because you can love your family and hate their guts at the same time. You may disagree with their values, dislike their friends, cringe at things they say, and do your best to avoid having to speak to them, but you still miss your siblings when they aren't around, and you are still upset if something bad happens to them.

Today, remember that some siblings have close relationships while others can't stand each other, and that's normal. There's no need to feel guilty about not liking your siblings.

Say Good-bye to Jealousy

I used to be jealous of just about every one of my friends. I was jealous because I thought they were prettier than I was, had cuter clothes, were more talented, had more guys calling them, and more people liked them. I finally realized that I felt like I was always falling short because I was being a follower. I played volleyball because my friends did, took the classes they were in, wore certain clothes because they liked them, and talked to guys they thought were cool. Instead of doing what I loved, I was trying to live up to their image.

Then I finally started doing my own thing. I discovered art and writing. I met new people and started talking to guys I liked, and I did activities that made me happy. When I started doing things I liked, not only did my jealous feelings go away, my friendships became much stronger.

Instead of trying to be a mirror image of your friends, be yourself. You will find that when you are living up to standards you have set for your own life, there is no need to compete with your friends.

A Life Lesson from Pooh

When I was a child, I loved Winnie the Pooh. I read all the Pooh stories, watched every cartoon, and even knew some of them word for word. As I grew older, many of my other childhood affections died away, but my love for that little yellow round bear only grew stronger. Pooh is timeless, and there is a lot of wisdom within that bear even though he is only "a bear of very little brain."

Once Pooh asked Owl to write "A Happy Birthday" on the present he was giving Eeyore for his birthday. Pooh said he wasn't able to do it himself because "my spelling is Wobbly. It's good spelling but it Wobbles, and the letters get in the wrong places." We'd say that wobbly spelling with the letters in the wrong places isn't good spelling at all, yet Pooh believed in himself, and to him, his spelling was "good."

Maybe your hair doesn't curl the way you'd like it to, you don't have straight A's, or you didn't make the varsity volleyball team. Instead of getting down on yourself for not being perfect, remember Pooh. You may not have a perfect life, but you sure do have a good one.

In June...

Get those wheels spinning! Ride a bike, go rollerblading, try skateboarding.

As the school year ends, make a photo collage of you and your friends and all the fun things you have done together since September.

Have an ice cream party. Get your favorite flavors and all the toppings for a terrific sundae—chocolate sauce, fruit, butterscotch, nuts, whipped cream. Invite all your friends over and eat ice cream all night!

June is the month for fresh strawberries, so make it a point to enjoy some.

More Than Just Dreams

I once had a dream that I was dating this guy at my school. Even though I barely knew the guy, the day after I had that dream, I started to have a crush on him. Another time I had a dream that my friend and I had a huge fight, and the next day I found myself feeling mad at her even though she hadn't done anything wrong.

Dreams can really affect our moods and thoughts, and they often set the tone for the day we are beginning. Have you ever had a nightmare that you just couldn't shake, or dreamt about something that was going to happen, only to have it eventually came true?

Tonight, put a pad of paper by your bed. When you wake up in the morning, take a few minutes to write down your dream in as much detail as you can remember. What is this dream telling you? How do you feel about it? Pay attention to what your dreams tell you about yourself, because they are powerful tools for discovering what's going on in your mind.

Getting Outside Help for a Friend in Trouble

Do you have a friend who's in serious trouble? Maybe she's pregnant and won't ask anyone for help or she's ruining her life with drugs. Or maybe she's extremely depressed and you're worried she might hurt or kill herself. It's hard to watch a friend get herself into trouble. You want to help but can't do anything because some problems are too big for teens to handle alone.

If you feel your friend has a serious problem and needs help, it's okay to talk to an adult. Go to a school counselor and explain the situation. Counselors are good to talk to because they are required by law to keep what you tell them confidential. If you feel comfortable, go to your parents or another adult that you trust. Ask them for advice about how you should handle the situation.

It can be hard to break the friendship code of secrecy, and you make your friend mad at you, but you must do what you feel in your heart is right. You may feel that talking to an adult is ratting on your friend, but sometimes, in the long run, keeping quiet will hurt your friend more.

It's Graduation Time

The end of the school year is coming near, and soon you will be graduating. Sure, you may not be a senior graduating from high school, but you are still graduating. Do you remember how excited you were when you graduated from kindergarten because it meant that you were becoming more grown up?

Life is full of graduations and opportunities for learning and changing yourself. Finishing with one grade and moving on to the next marks an important transition in life. It shows you have gained another year of knowledge and are ready to take on new, more difficult challenges. Be excited today. Whether you are graduating from sixth grade, eighth grade, or high school, you are growing up and moving on to a new phase of your life.

Give Life Meaning with Love

"Unless you love something, nothing else makes sense," the poet e. e. cummings once said. Love gives our lives meaning and makes us excited to get out of bed in the morning. To love something is essential. Love fills your heart, makes you joyful, gives you a purpose, and raises your self-esteem. We girls often get confused and think that the "something" needs to be a guy. We equate love with having a boyfriend.

Love doesn't mean being in a relationship, and having something to love can be better than having somebody to love. Today, find something you love. Maybe it's gardening, working on your computer, writing stories, baby-sitting, cooking, or playing tennis. You can love anything, as long as you love something!

The Shadow of Your Siblings

Do you ever feel like you are in the shadow of your siblings? Like your parents favor one of you over the other? Maybe your sister is really intelligent or an amazing athlete, or your brother is an incredible musician. You may feel like no matter what you do, you can't live up to the standards they have created. It can be heartbreaking to feel that you have to compete for the love and attention of your parents.

When you are feeling frustrated by seemingly perfect siblings, remember that you are an individual. Instead of spending your time trying to follow in their footsteps, follow your own path. Just because you come from the same family doesn't mean you'll all have the same interests. Chase your own dreams! It may be difficult for you to step out of the path your siblings have paved, but you will feel wonderful when you are doing something that *you* love. In addition, your parents will be as proud of you for doing what you love as they are of your siblings for doing what they love.

If You Don't Like 'Em, Ignore 'Em

You don't like Emily; everything about her drives you crazy. You have absolutely no qualms about telling everyone how much you hate her, and when she's around, you go out of your way to make her feel uncomfortable.

You will not like everyone, and some people will irritate you so badly that you will absolutely hate them. That's okay, but it *isn't* okay to treat people cruelly, no matter how much you dislike them. Think about how you feel when people go out of their way to be mean to you—why would you want to hurt another person like that?

The best way to deal with someone you don't like is to be indifferent; don't be fake and pretend to like them, but don't go out of your way to be mean either. If they do something that bothers you, simply bite your tongue and ignore it.

Did You Ever Know That You're Their Hero?

A friend once told me that when he was a child, he wanted to marry his older sister. "You wanted to marry her?" I laughed. "Yep. She was so nice to me and I totally looked up to her. I thought she was the coolest girl ever."

Your younger siblings admire you more than you may realize. They look to you to see how they should act, talk, and treat others. In their eyes, you are the coolest, smartest, most fun, and most inspirational person they know, and the younger they are, the more they idolize you.

Think about how much fun they have when you let them tag along, how happy they are when you are nice to them, or how much they cherish the gifts you give them. You are their hero, even though they can be pests, get into your stuff, and call you names. So treat your younger siblings with care, because, believe it or not, you are their ultimate role model.

Clean Up Emotional Messes

It's time to bring the school year to an end, to get all your homework turned it, tests taken, books returned, and lockers cleaned out. Everything must be finished and your slate must be wiped clean. Before you jet out the door for the summer sun, have you gotten all of your emotional messes worked out? Have you had problems with certain friends throughout the year, or did you get onto a teacher's bad side by talking too much and not turning in your homework on time?

Clear up things before summer starts. Call a truce with an ex-boyfriend, send an apology to someone whose feelings you hurt, let the girl who used to be your best friend know that even though you grew apart the past year, you still care about her. Say and do whatever you feel is necessary. It's important to clear everything up so you can relax and enjoy your summer without having to worry about what's going to happen when you return to school in the fall.

Sitting Around Waiting for Him to Call

There is one truth about boys that rarely fails: they don't call when they say they will, no matter how much they seem to like you or how much fun you have on your first date. We give a guy our number, we sit, we wait, we turn down offers to go to the mall with friends, we stay within hearing distance of the phone at all times, and we pray. When he doesn't call, we feel rejected, let down, and annoyed.

The next time you're expecting a guy to call, try this trick: Don't stop your life just to wait for the phone to ring. Hang out with friends, do your homework, cook dinner with your family, and go about your normal day. If he doesn't call, you won't feel like you wasted your time for nothing. Keep your cool, and remember, to a guy, calling you just to talk seems unnecessary, not because he doesn't like you, but because it just isn't in his nature.

My Friends Are Making Fun of My Boyfriend

"Why does your boyfriend do his hair like that?" Megan asked me.

I looked over and saw that Ryan's hair did look kind of funny. "He likes it that way, I guess," I answered, feeling embarrassed by my friend's disapproval.

That wasn't the end of my friends making fun of Ryan—they told me he walked funny, his jeans were too tight, and he said dorky things. I liked Ryan a lot, but when my friends made fun of him, I started to think that maybe he wasn't as cute as I thought he was and maybe I shouldn't be with him.

Your friends won't always approve of the guy you like. They may make fun of him or even get into fights with him. Don't let their comments discourage you from spending time with a guy you like. Tell your friends that you really like this guy and that their actions are hurting your feelings. You never know why they're saying mean things; maybe they're jealous of the time you spend with him, or maybe they want you to like a friend of the guys they like. Remember, you don't need your friends' stamp of approval.

Make No Assumptions When Getting Physical

My junior year in high school, I dated a guy named Brian. We were making out on the couch one night when his parents were gone, and he said to me, "Let's go to my room. I've got a condom up there."

I was so shocked, I didn't know how to respond. Until that moment, I had assumed that everyone knew I was a virgin and that I was very adamant about waiting to have sex. Brian and I had gone to school together since kindergarten; I knew his family, his hobbies, what he looked like before he got his glasses and braces off, and every girl he had ever dated. Knowing me, how could he possibly think that I would have sex with him?

When it comes to getting physical with guys, make no assumptions. No matter how well you know them or think they know you, you should always make your feelings clear before you're in the middle of something that's hard to stop.

Search for Roots of the Argument

"I hate this song," I said, changing the radio station as Allison and I drove along.

"Turn it back," she said. "I like that song."

"What? You've always hated this song."

Allison flipped the radio back. "I changed my mind. Not everyone shares your musical taste."

"Whatever!" I argued. "You always have to be in control of the radio."

Our radio squabble kept Allison and me from speaking to each other for two weeks! When you find yourself becoming enraged over something that normally wouldn't upset you, it's a sign of deeper hurt feelings. When you get furious at your friend for not calling you back when she said she would, you're not really mad at her for calling late. You may feel she's been ignoring you lately.

Ask yourself what's really going on. What incidents have led to you blowing up over this? Arguments are weeds in the garden of friendship; you can cut off the tops, but unless you pull out the roots, they will continue to grow back.

I Love Being a Girl

We are the children of feminism, the products of a movement to create strong-minded women. In the mix of bra burning, girl power, and equality, we seem to have forgotten that *feminine* is the root of feminism. We are told to be strong and that being called "girly" is a criticism. Can't strength and girly-ness harmoniously coexist?

Of course they can! Being feminine doesn't mean you're an airhead. Girls have the best of both worlds: we can love to climb mountains, shoot baskets, build cars, or become scientists, and still pamper ourselves, paint our nails, curl our hair, or wear skirts. Celebrate being a girl. Be strong, intelligent, athletic, *and* do whatever it is that makes *you* feel beautiful.

Admire Your Friends

As teenage girls, we spend so much time competing with and being jealous of our girlfriends that we forget to recognize all the things we love about them. Focusing only on the negative aspects of your friendships may leave you wondering, "Why am I with these people?"

Today, make a list of your friends' good qualities. Write down everything that you admire and appreciate about your friends—how one is a hard worker, one is very athletic, and another is nice to everybody. What do your friends do for you? Maybe one always knows how to make you laugh, one always listens to you when you are down, and another always compliments your accomplishments.

Listing your friends' wonderful traits will help you remember why you became friends in the first place. It also reminds you that since such outstanding girls choose to be friends with you, you must be extremely outstanding, too.

Spending Time with Good Old Dad

Dads can be hard to figure out. When girls are young, their fathers are usually very active in their lives. As they grow out of girlhood and become teens, dads aren't quite sure of their place in their daughters' lives anymore. There is so much talk about the importance of building strong relationships between teenage girls and their mothers, but little talk of the importance of father–daughter relationships.

With Father's Day coming soon, do something special for your father. Make a date to hang out with Dad, just the two of you. How can you let him in on your interests while doing something he'll enjoy? Maybe you love art, so take him to the art museum to show him your favorite artists and then have lunch at his favorite restaurant. If your dad loves to do woodwork, suggest that the two of you build new bookshelves in your room. Find something the two of you can share, and don't let your relationship with your father fall by the wayside.

Clear Your Karma

Whenever my mother and I go to the mall, the movies, or any other place we know we'll have a difficult time finding a place to park, my mom always says, "Clear your parking karma." Together, we take a deep breath and visualize a parking spot. Without fail, every time we clear our "parking karma" together, we find a good space, not one way in the back of the parking lot.

When a challenging situation arises, whether it's trying to find a parking spot in a crowded lot, taking a test, or running in a track meet, you must clear your thoughts. Close your eyes, take a deep breath, and as you exhale, let all your negative ideas about your situation leave your mind. Visualize your challenge working perfectly, or working out even better than you could have planned. Believe me, when you clear your karma, good things will happen.

Getting Your Parents to Like Your Friends

You have a new friend whom you really like. She's very different from your other friends, and the two of you have a ton of fun together. There's just one problem—your parents don't like her, and they don't let you hang out with her as much as you'd like to.

If you find yourself in this situation, ask yourself, "Why don't my parents like my friend?" Has your friend done something that offends your parents? Do they have a valid reason for not liking her? I have found that my mom is usually right about my friends—if she doesn't like somebody, I usually don't end up being very good friends with that person.

If you really feel your parents haven't given your friend a chance, try writing a letter to them explaining why you like her. Tell them you feel they have unfairly judged her, and ask them what would get them to like the friend more. Your life will be much easier if you put in the effort to get your parents to like your friends.

Rest Your Emotional Injuries

When you have a physical injury, you give your body time to rest and recover. What happens when you have an emotional trauma, like your boyfriend breaking up with you, getting into a fight with friends, or having somebody close to you die? Have you ever noticed that emotional upsets affect both your emotional and physical well-being?

Think about how you feel when you have an emotional trauma. Does your stomach feel sick or your head hurt? You may find your appetite changes drastically, you feel exhausted, slow, and unable to think clearly. Whenever I am very upset, the only thing I can think to do is crawl into bed and sleep.

When you have an emotional trauma, you need to give your body just as much time to recover as you give your feelings. Take it easy, slip into a warm bath, take a gentle walk, and get plenty of rest. The more you take care of yourself during a difficult emotional time, the sooner your heart and body will be back in tip-top shape.

Be Direct

Your boyfriend is going on vacation tomorrow for two weeks, and you really want him to call you while he's gone, but you aren't sure if he will or not. What do you do? Drop subtle hints, and then cross your fingers, hoping that he calls? The best thing to do is ask him directly, "Will you please call me while you are on vacation?"

I used to think that asking for what you want in relationships was a bad thing. I thought if somebody cared about me then they should be able to figure out what I wanted and do it without me having to ask them. People aren't mindreaders, and unless you say exactly what you want, they will never know.

Today, stop dropping hints and start asking for what you want from your relationships. Tell your friend you wish she would invite you to hang out with her more often, or ask your boyfriend to stop making fun of you in public. If they make an effort to do what you ask, you will know you are an important person in their lives.

He Knows I Like Him

You have a crush on Austin, and the only two friends who know were sworn to secrecy. That's why you're completely shocked when his best friend comes up to you at lunch and says, "I hear you like Austin."

Okay, so the guy of your dreams has found out your true feelings for him; there's no need to freak out. Keep your cool. Instead of turning bright red and yelling, "I never said I liked him!" take a deep breath and say, "Austin's cool." You don't have to admit anything, and you don't have to deny anything. The calmer you stay about the situation, the sooner people will stop teasing you about your crush.

Who knows, maybe he has liked you all along, and finding out that you like him is just the boost he needs to ask you out.

Lighten Up

Imagine if everyone took life seriously all the time and never told jokes or teased a little bit—everything would be heavy, dark, and depressing.

Today, live lightheartedly. Don't get worked up if someone says something mean about you, just take it as a joke and laugh it off. Instead of getting embarrassed at your parents' laughing loudly in public, laugh with them. If you get a bad grade on a test, shrug it off. Life is too important to always be taken so seriously, and if you are always solemn, you will miss opportunities to have fun and be spontaneous.

Oh, the Pains of Pimples

"Sick!" my friend yelled, pointing at my face. "You have the biggest zit on your chin! That is so gross!"

I threw my hand over my chin, my face turning bright red. "I do?"

"Yes, it is huge. Yuck!" I ran into the bathroom to examine my face. She was right! When did that thing get there? It wasn't there when I left for school this morning. What was I going to do now? I imagined that for the rest of the day people would be staring at my chin and I would be known as the girl with the zit. How embarrassing! How could this happen to me?

Pimples are pains. They always come at the worst times and make you feel extremely self-conscious as you worry that everyone is going to notice your blemish. Other than applying tropical creams and cover-ups, there isn't much you can do about pimples but wait for the little buggers to leave on their own. The wonderful thing about pimples is that we all get them, and eventually they do go away.

Go for It!

What do you want to do? Is there an experience you long for, like studying art in Italy, working as a summer camp counselor, or learning to rock climb?

Go do it! The world is full of opportunities, more than your parents ever had at your age. There is someone out there who can help you do whatever you want to do. Just because you don't know of any school programs for teens in Italy doesn't mean they don't exist. Go to the library, surf the Web, and talk to teachers; if you put your heart in it, you will find more opportunities than you ever dreamed.

If there is something you are dying to do, go for it! Just because nobody you know has done it doesn't make it impossible. Just because it isn't something that's considered "normal" for teens to be doing doesn't mean that it isn't worthwhile. Go ahead and travel beyond your comfort zone or the bubble of your town to do something you have always dreamed of. You can do it!

A Day of Gratitude

Everyone has many reasons to feel grateful—what are yours? Maybe it's your supportive family, your best friend who is a ton of fun, a wonderful pet, or being able to play your favorite sport. Today, make a list of the things you are thankful for. Who has helped to make your day run smoothly? What things have made you happy? Even if you are having a terrible day, there are still many things to be thankful for, like the sunshine, or someone holding open a door for you when your hands are full.

Be observant, and you will see just how much you have to be thankful for. Whether it's a person or an object, an action, or a thought, big or small, recognize all the good things that are happening in your life.

My Parents Are Getting a Divorce

My parents got divorced when I was very young, too young to remember. As a teen, I was happy about that because I watched many friends go through the pain of seeing their parents separate. When your parents decide to get a divorce, it tears apart your entire family. You may find yourself feeling forced to take sides, or trying to patch up your parents' broken marriage.

If there has ever been a time when it has been necessary for you to look out for your own best interests, now is that time. No matter what you do, you will never be able to fix your parents' problems. The most important thing for you now is to do what is best for you. Talk to a school counselor or a family member who is willing to listen and give you honest advice. Seek out a friend whose parents have been through a divorce and see how he or she handled it.

Today, turn your attention to yourself and try to find a way that you can be happy with your parents' divorce.

I'm a Tormented Teen, Too

Do you ever feel like nobody understands you? Like others just don't *get* it, and you are the only one who *really* sees the world clearly? Is your life ever full of anguish, and do you ever get the sense you are suffering all alone? You may be lonely and feel like nobody notices your accomplishments or appreciates your individuality. You are full of inner angst, turmoil, and suffering in ways that no other person could ever understand.

Guess what—everyone feels this way. You are not the first, nor will you be the last "tormented teen." Holden Caulfield, the protagonist of J. D. Salinger's novel *Catcher in the Rye*, is a classic tormented teen. So are Claire Dane's character, Angela, on *My So-Called Life* and Daria, the alienated cartoon teen with her own show. We are all a little tormented; it goes along with the territory of being a teen. Just remember that as bad as you feel, you've got a lot of company.

Don't Tease Me

I'm not very good at being teased because I take everything very personally. When people tease me about my rosy cheeks or something embarrassing I did, I am hurt. When people make fun of me, even in a light-hearted way, I feel like they are pointing out my faults, and I become defensive and devastated.

If you also have a hard time being the butt of any joke, the best thing you can do is learn how to be teased. Today, try not to get worked up or defensive when somebody makes fun of you. Laugh it off and don't take it to heart. The less attention you give a person when they are bothering you, the sooner they will stop doing it. If it is a friend who is teasing you, and she continues to tease you about something that hurts your feelings, ask her to stop making you the butt of her jokes.

Summer School

The nursery rhyme my friends and I used to sing on the last day before summer vacation in elementary school goes like this: "No more classrooms, no more books. No more teachers' dirty looks!" It was a song of relief celebrating our escape from obligation and moving into summer where we were free from bedtimes and could play as much as we wanted.

Now that you are out of school, sharpening your mind probably isn't on the top of your list. Summer actually is the perfect time for learning. It's fun to learn when there are no deadlines, papers, tests, or lectures, and when you are just focusing on something that sparks *your* interest.

Expand your mind this summer. What have you always wanted to know more about? Spend a day at the library collecting topics that get your knowledge flame burning. When you are in charge, the possibilities are endless, and your classroom can be anywhere.

Ditch the classroom and teachers this summer, but keep the books. You will find that learning for yourself will bring you joy that school never can.

Travel around the World

When I was fifteen, my mother and I went to Indonesia. I'd never been out of the country, and during our flight, I wrote in my journal, "I have no idea what to expect. Will they have electricity and running water? What will their streets and houses look like? I'm nervous that I will hate it and that it will be scary there!" My fears were put at ease the minute I walked off the plane. It was nothing like America, and for that reason I loved it even more; it was tropical and exotic. I learned more on that two-week trip than I had in my previous nine years of schooling.

Traveling broadens your world. It exposes you to things you never knew existed, things you could never learn sitting in a classroom. Today, take a trip to another part of the world. You can't hop on a plane and fly to another country, but you can pick up a book and discover a new land. What will you do while you're there? What will you see and learn? What is the culture like? Make an itinerary for a trip that lasts as long as your heart desires.

Remember Your Grandparents

My grandmother took me shopping for a new outfit, and at one store she saw a tank top that said "spoiled" across the front. She immediately bought it for me because it describes exactly what she does to me—my grandma has spoiled me rotten since I can remember, and I love it!

Grandparents are wonderful to have around. They brag to all their friends about you, show off your latest picture to anyone who may want to see it, give you love and comfort, and if you're lucky, spoil you rotten. Without the responsibility of raising you, they have freedom to love you with fewer restrictions than your parents have.

Let your grandparents know that you appreciate them by sending them a card or calling them. Don't become so carried away with your everyday life that you forget to recognize the older people who think, as my grandfather would say, "you are the greatest thing since sliced bread."

In July...

Make big salads, and enjoy all the fresh fruits that summer brings.

Read a classic novel. Try The Great Gatsby, The Adventures of Huckleberry Finn, Emma, *or* A Separate Peace.

Run through the sprinkler, jump in a pool, or swim in the ocean.

Who Are You?

Here's some simple advice that's often hard for teens to follow: Just be you. You don't need to pretend, think about what you will say, or imitate someone else. All you have to do is behave like you. You can only do this, however, if you truly know yourself.

During her adventures in Wonderland, when Alice is asked by the caterpillar, "Who are you?" she responds, "I hardly know, Sir, just at present. At least I know who I *was* when I got up this morning, but I think I must have been changed several times since then." Alice has it right. Your body, emotions, thoughts, experiences, surroundings, friends, hopes, and dreams are changing at a rapid pace.

Today, spend one hour with yourself walking or just sitting in your room. Don't think about other people or the work you have to do, just think about you. Carry on a conversation—how are you feeling, what happened today, what do you hope for tomorrow? Spend time getting to know the most important person in your life—you.

Celebrate Literacy

Today is National Literacy Day, so celebrate by enjoying a good book. Head for the library, your favorite bookstore, or even your own bookshelf, and pick a book. Reread a book you love. Some of my favorites are Lucy M. Montgomery's *Anne of Green Gables*, J. D. Salinger's *Catcher in the Rye*, and Lewis Carroll's *Alice's Adventures in Wonderland*. Get a book you've always wanted to read, or ask a friend to suggest one they enjoyed. Try a collection of short stories or a poetry anthology.

You grow a little bit with each book you read. It is wonderful to become so close to a character in a book that you'd like to sit down and have a conversation with him or her; so is finding something you can take from a book and apply to your own life. Today, celebrate your ability to read.

Summertime Is My Time

Summer provides the perfect opportunity to do things you enjoy. There is no school, no homework, and no extracurricular activities. With all this free time on your hands, what do *you* want to do?

This summer, make up for all the hours you spent studying or in class by spending twice as much time doing things you love. Do something *you* enjoy, not something your friends love, or something you feel you should like. Don't worry about having friends come along with you—this is something you can do for yourself. Play tennis every day, take a long walk in the park, swim, go outside and paint, or lay in a hammock all day.

Enjoy the freedom of summer by doing exactly what you want!

Treasure Chests

When our grandmothers were girls, they kept hope chests—large trunks full of linens, dishes, and other housewares they saved for when they got married. For our grandmothers, a wedding day was the day their lives began.

Grandma's hope chest is a wonderful thing, but it definitely needs some updating. You're not sitting around saving things or waiting to get married so your life can begin. Your life is already full of exciting experiences, so why not create your own treasure chest right now?

Find a large trunk or a big wooden box from a thrift shop and decorate it in a way that reflects your personality. Use bright colors or floral patterns, and line the inside with wallpaper or soft fabric. Fill your chest with things that are important to you. Capture memories by putting in pictures, letters, and your scrapbooks. Add poetry, artwork, stories, and quotes that touch your heart. Put pictures of the exotic places you hope to visit during your life, and the other dreams you have for your future.

Your treasure chest will become a reflection of you and something you can cherish always.

My Dream Day

Today is your dream-come-true day! Just for a day, imagine there are no roadblocks, no restrictions, nothing to hold you back. You can do anything, because this is your day to do exactly what you want. Walk on the beach, ride a horse through the mountains, travel to Italy, or win an Oscar. The possibilities are endless!

Picture yourself gliding through the ocean on a beautiful sailboat, or being pampered from head to toe at a spa in Hawaii. Write about your perfect day in your journal. What are you wearing, who are you with, and what sounds, sights, and smells are around you? Let your mind run free—your only requirement is making your day a perfect one from beginning to end.

So you may not have enough money to travel to Europe right now, and you haven't starred in a movie to win that Oscar. Other people have their dreams come true all the time, so why shouldn't you? The more you imagine your perfect day, the sooner it will come true!

Start Pedaling

Contrary to popular belief, the car is not the best form of travel. A *bike* is the best way to get around. Have you ever taken your bike for a long ride? It is so wonderful to travel with the fresh air all around you and the sun shining on your face. Your bike can get you where you need to go, and it's a great way to exercise. You can get a new perspective of your hometown when you're on a bike.

Next time you need something at the store or want to go to visit a friend, hop on your bike and start pedaling!

Family Vacation Time

It's that time again—the annual family vacation. You are anything but excited. You've tried to get out of it, saying, "There really isn't any point in spending so much money on a vacation when we have a beautiful home right here." Or, "Who's going to water the flowers? Out of the kindness of my heart, I'll miss out on the vacation to stay home and do it." Or begging: "Please let me stay home!" Even your best efforts failed.

The mere thought of spending a week in close quarters with your quirky family may drive you crazy, but since you have no choice, it's in your best interest to make the most of the situation. Pretend you are in a movie, like *National Lampoon's Family Vacation*. Be lighthearted, entertain yourself, and laugh at your family instead of letting them irritate you.

No matter how jolly you are, there will be times when you'll feel overloaded by too much family time. Instead of blowing up, release your frustrations by taking a walk by yourself or writing in your journal. The better attitude you have, the easier your trip will be. You may even find yourself having a good time.

Find a Nature Spot

Do you have a spot in nature? A place you like to relax and feel connected to the outdoors? Having a nature space that speaks to you is important, because there is something magical about the outdoors that calms, inspires, and rejuvenates your spirit.

Today, find a piece of nature you can connect with. Sit under a tree in your backyard, climb a mountain peak, lie on the sandy beach near the ocean, or paddle a boat around the lake. Make this your sacred nature spot, get to know it well, and take care of it. Go there to read, draw, daydream, or simply have some time alone. You will get a great deal of comfort from that little spot.

Make a Tape of Your Voice

When I was a child, my mom would tape-record herself reading my favorite bedtime stories and then give me these tapes. I loved those tapes; I listened to them at night when I went to bed and took them with me to summer camp. I still have a few in my dorm room that I listen to whenever I need some comforting.

Tapes of your voice make excellent gifts for people you love. Maybe your friend is going on vacation for the summer; make her a tape with you telling funny stories in between your favorite songs. Maybe your parents are divorced and you live far away from your mother; record yourself talking about what you've been up to lately and have your brothers and sisters talk on it as well. You can make a tape for your grandparents, your boyfriend, or your siblings, or for special occasions, or just because. There is nothing as comforting as hearing the voice of a person you love.

Wanting Freedom

It's summer! You want to be free to go wherever your desires may call: playing at the beach all day, staying up all night with your girlfriends talking with the boys you just met, or spending a lazy afternoon lounging in your hammock and sipping lemonade. All this could be true, but there's just one thing holding you back—your parents. Their school year rules don't seem to allow much room for carefree summertime plans.

If you feel you need a little more independence, it's time to put in a rule-change request. Instead of arguing, write out a petition that states the change you would like (a midnight curfew instead of eleven) and then explains your reason (you like to stay up later in the summer because you don't have to get up early for school). Give it to your parents and ask them to be open-minded as they read it over. Then make an appointment to discuss your request. My suggestion is waiting a week so that they have had enough time to think it over.

Even if your request isn't granted, you will have earned major brownie points for approaching your parents in a mature way.

Be Lazy

My favorite way to bask in the summer is spending a day lying in my hammock, sipping lemonade, listening to music, or reading a book and napping in between chapters. Summer isn't summer without at least a few days of laziness.

Today, turn your brainpower down to minimum and shift gears to summer-speed. Lounge by the pool, read a pleasure book, or lie in bed all day. Remember—it's summer!

Perk Up with a Song

One year at summer camp, we were split up into different groups for camp duties. I got stuck doing my absolute least favorite chore—washing dishes. Instead of griping, I decided that since I had no choice, I had better make it fun. I started a sing-along with the dishwashing group. Together we washed the dishes and sang our favorite songs. We had such a blast singing that we were even a little sad every night when the dishes were all clean. Pretty soon everyone saw how much fun we were having, and during chore time the camp was filled with song.

Today make "have-to's" fun by remembering the motto of Snow White and the Seven Dwarfs: "Whistle while you work." Work is always fun with music because it's impossible to be in a bad mood while you're singing.

Your Best Friend's New Friend

Ellen's your best friend, and she has a new friend, Stacy, whom you can't stand. Stacy's been coming along with you and Ellen to the movies, joining you for lunch, and Ellen also invited Stacy to spend the night even though it was just supposed to be you two. Stacy gets on your nerves, and you don't know how much more you'll be able to take.

Before you do something drastic, think. Do you really dislike Stacy, or is it just that she's spending time with your best friend? Whether it is one reason or a combination of both, you're going to have to learn to live with the new friend if you want to keep your best friend. Your best friend has the right to be friends with whomever she chooses. The worst thing you can do is put her in a position where she has to choose between you two, because that will make her pull away from you.

If you really have a hard time getting along with your best friend's new friend, the next time you three are supposed to hang out, invite another person to come along so you'll have another person to talk to.

I Don't Care, What Do You Want to Do?

Have you ever tried to make plans with a guy and had this conversation?

"What should we do?" he asks.

"I don't really care. I'm up for anything," you reply.

"Well, we could rent a movie and watch it at my house, or we could go out to a movie."

"Either sounds good, so whatever you want."

"I want to do both, so you decide."

We're often afraid to express our opinions to guys because we're afraid our ideas will be rejected. You don't say what movie you really want to see because you're afraid he'll think it's stupid, or you keep quiet instead of telling him you like Mexican food better than Italian. Even if you really don't care about what you do, it's better to choose something than to sit and vacillate all night long.

Express your opinion. Being wishy-washy causes more problems than when you just say what you want. Most likely the guy is trying to think of something you like to do, so just tell him and keep the decision making easy for both of you.

For the Love of Tanning

The sun is shining, and your main mission is to be completely tan by the time school starts. Think again. I've always been a huge advocate of protecting my skin. Whenever I go to the beach with friends, I wear a hat and sun block, or sit in the cool shade of a tree. I play "mom" and always remind my friends, "Put on sunscreen. You'll be thankful when you're older and don't have wrinkles or skin cancer!" Often they reply, "I don't care about when I'm older. I want to be tan while I'm young," which sparks the adult in me to say, "The longer you stay out in the sun, the sooner you're going to look old!"

Wear sunscreen. Are you really willing to risk permanent skin damage for one little tan? I know you've heard it before, but I'm telling you again, having a tan is a sign of skin damage. You're only a teenager for seven years of your life, and you will thank yourself later if you protect your skin now.

Write a Letter

I never realized what a wonderful thing e-mail was until I went to college. With the push of a few keys on my keyboard, I can keep in touch with my mom at home, my friends at schools all over the country, and even my friends who are studying abroad. It is so simple and makes being away from people I care about easier.

As wonderful as e-mail is, it can never replace the excitement of receiving a letter. A handwritten letter is so personal and so heartfelt. You are brought closer to your friend when you see her handwriting. I can already see myself saying to my grandchildren, "I remember before e-mail when we had to write letters by hand that had to be delivered by mailmen, and it took a few days to send them where we wanted them to go."

Keep the dying form of letter writing alive. Write to your grandparents or to a friend who has moved away, or make a pen pal. Cherish the letters you receive because someday you will reread them with fondness.

Get Outside and Move

After I've spent an entire day inside, I always feel crabby and in a daze. My brain hurts, I can't think clearly, and I'm lethargic. I need to rejuvenate.

Whether you've spent all day at work, watching television, studying for summer school, or just lazing around the house, going outside and moving around will give you an energy boost. Spending an entire day without physical activity makes your body feel heavy, your thoughts slow, and can put you in a rotten mood.

Go for a bike ride, take a walk around your neighborhood, or jump in the water for a swim. If you make time to get outside and move around, you will be able to work harder, think more clearly, be in a better mood, and have much more energy to do fun things that you love.

Picking Up on Guys

One summer day, my two best friends and I took a trip to a tiny windsurfing town on the Columbia River. As we checked into our hotel, we met a guy our age and made plans to meet him and his two friends that night for pizza. We were thrilled—what's a summer vacation without boys?

My attitude toward summer romances changed quickly when I realized that, without having any say, I was being paired with the guy who shoved rolled pieces of toilet paper up his nose to stop it from bleeding.

This is the story of my life when it comes to meeting new guys. Have you ever noticed that in every group of guys, no matter how cute, fun, or friendly they are, there's always one who is a little off? He's the one I would be stuck with. It always left me wondering, "Does this make me the dorky girl in my group? Am I so uninteresting and ugly that none of the other guys want me?"

Remember that when guys pick up on a group of girls, it's for superficial reasons. Don't judge your self-worth on whether or not the "good" guys notice you.

Throw a Party

Feeling bored? Throw a party! They're fun to plan and can be low-key and mellow or loud and crazy. Whether you have five people or twenty, a party is a perfect cure for your midsummer blues.

The most original parties are theme parties. Ask your girlfriends if they want to help you plan a party, and then brainstorm ideas that would be fun. Have a barbecue and set up a volleyball net, horseshoe pit, and croquet game in your yard; organize a party to play a huge game of "Capture the Flag" or "Hide and Seek"; or throw a big dance party at your house. Whatever you host, make sure it has your style and character. An original party is sure to be fun for all.

Try a Spa Party

Get the girls together for a good old-fashioned slumber party, but with a twist. Invite whomever you'd like, and ask every girl to wear comfortable pajamas and bring their favorite beauty essential—nail polish, a facial mask, avocado facial scrub, a sweet-smelling lotion, cucumbers for the eyes, or hot rollers.

Make sure you have plenty of good food on hand, like cut veggies, fruit, finger sandwiches, and, of course, ice cream. Put on great music and spend the whole night pampering yourselves. Wash your faces, paint your nails, curl your hair, and try new makeup. You can always do the usual slumber party activities like prank-calling the boys and watching horror movies. There is no bonding like slumber party bonding!

How About a Mystic Night Party?

Everyone loves to have their fortune told—what better way to do it than with a mystic night party? Get some of your closest friends together and go to the library to learn about different fortune-telling tools, like tarot cards, runes, palm reading, and zodiac signs. Each of you can become an expert in one of the areas. At your party, you will show off your new talent by telling your guests about their futures and personalities, and helping them with problems they are having.

Have a crystal ball, dim the lights, put on mysterious music, and serve fortune cookies for snacks. Throwing a mystic party is an original way to have fun and get to know more about your friends.

Turning Siblings into Friends

I am an only child and am always jealous of people who aren't. "If I had brothers and sisters, I would never fight with them," I'd think as I watched my friends war with their siblings.

It's probably easier said than done, but take this advice from a lonely only: appreciate your siblings. Sometimes you may wonder how you could come from the same family because you have absolutely nothing in common with your siblings, but that doesn't mean you have to be enemies.

Today, make an effort to get along with your siblings. Take a deep breath if they start to annoy you. Instead of yelling, talk nicely to them like you'd talk to a friend, and be willing to lend a hand when they ask for your help. Although it won't happen overnight, building a relationship with your siblings will be well worth your efforts. A family has a bond that can never be replicated by friends, so cherish it.

Be a Stargazer

As a child I always wanted to see a UFO. My friends and I used to sit outside in my backyard, staring into space, hoping an alien ship would fly by. Although my wish didn't come true, I still love to gaze into the night sky and imagine all that lies far out in our universe.

Today marks the beginning of UFO Days, and whether or not you believe in visitors from space, it's always fun to be a stargazer. Get a book on constellations, grab your friends, and head for a place where you can see the stars. Search for your favorite constellations, wish on shooting stars, tell spooky stories of aliens, and contemplate what's going on in outer space.

Listen to Your Soul

People often say that taking care of our mind, body, and soul gives us a balanced life. Keeping your mind healthy means continually keeping your brain engaged by reading and challenging yourself to learn, and keeping your body healthy means following a well-balanced diet and exercising, but how does a girl keep her soul healthy?

Your soul is the part inside that feels amazed by the sunrise, cries during sad movies, and is touched by the sound of beautiful music. It's the part of you that gets excited about living, about waking up on a sunny morning, and about laughing really hard with your friends.

Today, pay attention to your soul. How is your soul doing? When you feel stressed, excited, happy, or sad, take a deep breath and listen to your soul. Hear what your soul is saying. What signals is it sending you? What is it telling you to do? Your soul reflects your attitude about life, and learning to listen to it will help make your outlook on life healthy.

Follow Your Heroes

What do you want to do when you "grow up"? If you could have any career you wanted, what would you do? Would you be an astronaut, fashion designer, professional golfer, doctor, or movie producer? Today, find an adult who has your dream job. If you can't meet someone personally, learn all you can about his or her career and how he or she got that particular job.

Follow your heroes and discover what they were doing at your age that helped get them to the places they are today. Write letters, ask questions, and learn all you can about the people who have the career you would like to have someday. Remember that every successful adult was once a teenager like you, and there's no reason you can't be the next Madonna, Oprah, or even Bill Gates.

Just One More Hour of Sleep

When I was in elementary school, I jumped out of bed promptly at seven every morning to make sure I had plenty of time to watch cartoons before I had to go to school. It seemed like when I turned thirteen, it was nearly impossible to drag myself out of bed to get to first period on time. I hated the sound of my alarm and always slept in as late as I possibly could.

Have you been having a hard time crawling out of bed in the morning, or are your parents constantly getting on your case about sleeping too late on the weekends? If you're beginning to love sleep, here's news for you: You're not lazy, you're normal. A recent study at Brown University showed that people need more sleep than ever during their teenage years, but also that teens have more energy at night. Your natural body rhythm keeps you up until two in the morning and asleep until noon the next day. You are growing, so be good to your body by giving it extra amounts of rest and sleep.

That's What I Like

Sometimes it may be hard for you to know what you like. There are so many different pressures—from the media and your peers—telling you what you should like that it's almost impossible to decide for yourself.

Start noticing what draws your interest and what activities turn you off. When your friends want to go see a movie, do you go because you're interested in the movie or because your friends want to go? Do you tell a friend you like a song just because you know she likes it? Friendships are built on common interests, but you and your friends don't have to like all the same things. Your friendships will be much stronger when you express your own interests and ideas instead of going along with what everyone else says.

Today, think about what you like. If you were to make a list of favorite things, what would be on it? What types of music, activities, movies, books, and food do you like? Where are your favorite places to go? What's your favorite time of day? Your favorite season? Use your journal to record what you like, and add to your list as you find more interests.

Make a Movie

My friends and I used to go crazy with the video camera. We would make movies and dance videos. We
recorded our slumber parties and our toilet paper
raids on the guys' houses. We recorded the school
assemblies we were in, our sporting events, and school
dances. We spent hours watching our homemade
videos, and we still bring them out when we get
together over college breaks and need a good laugh.

Make movies of you and your friends this summer.
If you don't have a video camera, maybe one of your
friends does, or try borrowing one from school.
Record yourselves doing funny things, dancing, getting ready to go out, or at parties. You will love looking
back and will crack up at all the crazy things you did.

"I've Become the Parent"

The teenage years are the time for growing up and slowly becoming an adult, but some teens are forced to grow up sooner than others. When your parents get a divorce, when a parent is very ill or dies, or when your parents have a drinking or drug problem, you may find that you have taken on the parental role in your family. Especially if you are the oldest, you may find that you've taken on responsibilities that your parents haven't been able to handle, like taking care of chores around the house and looking after your siblings. You've been forced to grow up more quickly than most of your peers.

Today, act your age and give yourself a chance to cut loose. Don't take on extra responsibilities or pick up where others have slacked off. You are a teen, and today is your day to act like it.

Be Nostalgic, Remember, and Reminisce

Have you noticed the happy feeling you have when you remember the good times you've shared with your friends? As William Shakespeare wrote in his play *Richard II*, "I count myself in nothing else so happy as in a soul remembering my good friends."

Today, be nostalgic and take time to remember all the wonderful things you have done with friends. Get out photos, scrapbooks, and mementos from the past. Reread your letters and old diaries. Look at how much you have grown and changed since then, even if it was only a few months ago. You'll smile when you see how many of your dreams came true, and how a situation that you thought was terrible actually turned out okay in the end. Think about past crushes, exciting times with friends, and fun vacations. You can always travel back in time; it's as simple as taking a trip down memory lane.

Take a Trip across Town

You're bored of your house, your neighborhood, and the area where you live. You are dying for some new scenery and a change of pace, but your family hasn't planned a vacation, and you are stuck in the same place all summer.

When I feel stuck in a rut and tired of the same old place, I take a trip. Of course I can't hop on a plane and fly around the world, but I can always travel to the other side of town, and so can you. If you don't drive, you can take the bus, ride your bike, or ask someone in your family with a car to drop you off and pick you up later. Go to your favorite part of town and pretend you are a tourist. Eat a good lunch, wander through the shops, sit and people-watch, or see a movie by yourself. Taking a trip across town is a wonderful cure for hometown boredom.

In August...

Make a summer slushy by putting your favorite fruit juice in a plastic container and put it in the freezer. Take it out just before it's completely solid for a delicious cooling treat.

Listen to reggae music.

Enjoy your last month of summer.

Take a Breather from Fights

One day, my mother and I got into our biggest fight. With red faces and tears pouring out of our eyes, we were both screaming at each other at the top of our lungs. Nothing was getting solved, and neither of us could think straight, so I left and walked to my friend's house. It was an hour-long walk, and by the time I got there, I had cooled down and was able to see things in perspective. I called my mom, and when she came to get me, we were able to work out the problem that had caused such an uproar earlier that day.

Sometimes when you are fighting with someone, the best thing to do is to back off. Give the other person space and take space for yourself so that you both can think about the situation and understand your own feelings. No fight has ever been solved during the heated passion of an argument. Go for a walk, write in your journal, or turn on loud music and scream. It's better to release your aggression so you don't say or do something that will hurt someone you care about.

Go Shopping in Your Own Closet

One of the things I loved most about going back to school was getting new school clothes. Adding new clothes to my closet excited me, and I would spend hours trying on my clothes, deciding on the perfect statement I wanted to make that first day of school.

While many of us would love to start off the school year with a brand new wardrobe, completely restocking the closet is expensive and out of the question for most of our budgets. The key is using your old clothes to make an exciting new wardrobe. Today, go shopping in your own closet. Get out your favorite clothes, dig out the clothes that have been hiding in the back, and put different pieces together to make outfits that you have never worn. Sometimes just mixing around your clothes will make them seem new, and you'll be surprised at how many fashion possibilities are hidden in the clothes you already have.

Spice Up Your Wardrobe

Spend today at the mall, not buying, but trying on, creating, and observing. Go into all your favorite stores and try on outfits that you love; don't let money be an object. What colors and styles catch your eye? Do you like skirts or pants? Which clothes fit your personality and make you feel the most comfortable and pretty? How about shoes and accessories—purses, jewelry, makeup? Make a list of all the clothes you love and remember to include the colors that you like best.

Now you are ready to hit the discount, second-hand, and consignment stores, and even garage sales. Look for clothes similar to those you tried on at the mall; you'll be surprised by how you can create almost identical outfits for much less.

Spicing up your wardrobe is fun and easy and doesn't have to be expensive. Just know your personal style and be smart about how you shop.

My Family's Ruining My Summer!

You've been out of school for a while now, enjoying the relaxation and freedom of summer. Even though you are virtually worry-free, your family may be getting on your nerves.

You may love them, but after six weeks of summer, they can drive you crazy. This time of year, my mother and I would be at each other's throats because we were used to the school year when I spent less time at home. Maybe your parents constantly remind you to do your chores or your little sister tags along wherever you go. Your once-relaxing summer has turned into a family war.

The summer madness isn't over yet; you have almost a month before school starts again. Think about how you can keep your family from driving you crazy. Get your chores done before your parents ask, tell your sister you'll take her to get ice cream if she stops pestering you.

Don't let family feuds ruin a perfect summer. Make an effort to get things running smoothly. If all else fails, you can always escape to the beach or pool!

You Are a Tulip

Imagine you are walking through a large green field. There isn't much around, just green grass and a few dandelions. Suddenly you come upon a bright pink tulip. Its beauty takes your breath away. Not yet fully bloomed, it stands alone, swaying ever so slightly in the breeze. How you love that flower and marvel at its remarkable color all day long!

The tulip knows it is the most beautiful thing in its field, but it isn't bragging or telling everything around it how great it is. The tulip doesn't try to change its form so it can blend in with the rest of the field; instead, it stands high and is happy. Value yourself as much as you value that rare pink tulip—you are as splendid, as vivid, and as bright.

Why Are You Mad at Me?

Your friend is mad at you. Maybe she's giving you the silent treatment and glares at you every time you walk past, or maybe she's talking behind your back and telling everyone terrible things about you. The worst part is that you don't even know what you did wrong.

Ask your friend to talk with you about her upset feelings. Write her a note explaining your confusion about what you've done wrong, and ask her if she'd be willing to get together and talk about it, or call her and try to work your situation out over the phone. If you find that your friend isn't willing to talk about the situation, it's a sign that she isn't the type of friend you want. Remember, a good friend will always want to work out problems and shouldn't get mad at you for no apparent reason.

Becoming a Culinary Master

Cooking can be an incredibly creative activity with a delicious reward at the end. The summer is the best time to become a culinary master because your taste buds are at their peak, fruits and vegetables are at their juiciest, and you actually have the time to enjoy cooking.

Today, plan a date to cook for your family. Look through cookbooks and put together a meal that excites you. Find something new that your family would enjoy, make a shopping list, and ask your parents to take you to the store. Invite your siblings to help, or make this meal on your own. Don't forget to include a delicious dessert!

Cooking dinner for your family will definitely be a positive experience. As writer Oscar Wilde said, "After a good dinner one can forgive anybody, even one's own relations."

Discovering Your Passion

Many say we humans are on a search for the meaning of life. We are searching for happiness, love, or a reason to get out of bed in the morning. As Bill Moyers puts it, we are seeking the experience of being alive. Do you ever notice that some days you feel more alive than others? Think of the moments when you love life, when you have a smile on your face that doesn't seem to fade, and when everything is working in your favor. These are the moments that create meaning in life; these things are your passions.

What makes you feel most alive? Is it music, art, sports, literature, nature, or people? Search for your passion, and when you discover it, indulge yourself as much as possible. When you discover your passion, you will give your life meaning.

One Final Summer Adventure

September is right around the corner, which means that you'll soon be spending six hours a day and five days a week in school. Your time will be devoted to school activities, homework, and sports, and you probably won't have much time for spontaneity. Now's the time to take one last summer adventure before hitting the books.

Round up your friends and do something out of the ordinary. Go on a picnic in the mountains, throw a beach party, spend a day at a water park, go horseback riding, or have a huge barbecue. What is that one thing that you and your friends have been talking about doing all summer but haven't gotten around to doing yet? It's the perfect time to do it, so seize the moment before the summer fades to autumn.

Breast Obsessed

My boobs started developing in the fifth grade. While other girls ran around carefree in tank tops, I tried desperately to hide my new developments. I wore baggy tee shirts with tight sports bras underneath, hoping to flatten my chest. I prayed for my boobs to go away, or for other girls to start getting them so I would feel normal.

When other girls' breasts started developing in junior high, mine were already a size B cup. A boy once asked me how much I weighed. When I told him 110 pounds, he said, "Yeah, well ten of that is your boobs!" I promised myself I'd get a breast reduction as soon as I could afford it.

Finding a swimsuit or a formal dress designed for a five-foot-tall girl with a size C chest isn't easy. I was baffled when a friend told me, "I wish I had your little body and big boobs!"

Boobs can be a real hassle. They get tender and swollen during your period and can draw unwanted attention on a cold day. Small, large, round, flat, we've all got 'em and, regardless of size or shape, we *all* wish they were different.

It's Hot!

It's hot: too hot to move and too hot to think. You're so hot you can't sleep at night or do much during the day. You're red-faced, sweaty, sticky, and crabby. All you want is for fall to hurry up so the days will be shorter and cooler.

The dog days of summer are well upon us. Today, make it your goal to keep cool. Eat popsicles, play in the sprinkler, take a cold shower, or sit in front of a fan with a cold towel on your face. Try putting cool cucumber slices on your eyes or put your lotion in the refrigerator to cool it before you put it on. When the dog days of summer get you down, make a few moments of cool to perk yourself back up.

Work That Sewing Machine

Did you know that the sewing machine was invented on August 12, 1851? Celebrate the invention that has helped make our favorite clothes and blankets by learning how to use a sewing machine.

Today, sew something. It doesn't have to be big or complicated. Ask your mom or grandmother for help. Get some material you like and sew a pillowcase, a tube top, a wrap-around skirt, or even a scarf for your hair. Learning to use a sewing machine could be well worth your time—just think how much fun it would be to make your own clothes! Even Donna Karan and Liz Claiborne had to start somewhere.

Parents Need a Lesson in Privacy

Has the word *privacy* seemed to have slipped out of your parents' vocabulary? Maybe your dad tries to listen in on your phone conversations, or you've caught your mom snooping through your drawers, though she insists she was just "putting your clothes away." Even Gladys Kravits, the busybody neighbor from *Bewitched*, is no match for your parents' meddlesome tactics.

It's time to request a plan for privacy guidelines in your house. Since you are their child, your parents may think everything you do is their business, but being your parents does not give them the right to go through your personal belongings without your permission.

Ask your parents to respect your personal space. Ask them not to go into your drawers, eavesdrop on your conversations, or read papers that are sitting on your desk. Assure them that you are not trying to keep major secrets from them, you just need to be allowed private space, thoughts, and time. Prevent them from snooping by acting in a way that is worthy of their trust.

Put an End to Friendship Rivalries

I once had a friend who was always competing with me. Whatever I did, she said she could do better. When I made a new friend, she would try to become a closer friend to that person. When I was having a bad day, she would insist that her day was worse. She didn't feel like a friend at all; she felt more like a rival.

One day when I was complaining about this, my mom said, "Stop competing with her." So I quit worrying about her attempts to outdo me, stopped letting her "I'm better than you" comments get me down, and started ignoring her competitive side. Lo and behold, she stopped competing with me.

Constantly being at odds with a friend is exhausting and hurtful. Today, stop letting competitive friends get you worked up. Drop out of the rivalry—remember, there will no longer be a competition if only one person is involved.

I'm Doing What I Say

I used to always say, "I can keep a secret because I am not a gossip." Then, in practically the same sentence, I would turn to my friends and say, "Did you hear about Christine and Gavin?" I was a hypocrite, and people knew it. They looked right through my declaration of how good I was at keeping my mouth shut and saw me for the gossip I really was.

Since then, I have learned the meaning of the saying, "Actions speak louder than words." Instead of going around telling everyone what you are, show them by your actions. People can easily spot hypocrisy, and they will make their judgments of you based on your actions, not on how you *claim* to act. Today, make sure that what you say and what you do match up.

We're All Deprived

I used to say that I was technology-deprived. Because I was living in a house without male influence, there were never any new or exciting gadgets. The one thing I longed for most was a big television. I wasn't asking for anything huge, just something larger than thirteen inches so that my friends and I could have movie nights at my house. My friends would joke, "If you want to watch TV at Amanda's, you'd better bring your binoculars!" I would tell my mom, "If there were a man in this house, we would have a better television!" We never got a big TV; in fact, we didn't even get cable until my sophomore year in high school. Finally I learned just to accept it—we were never going to have a big television.

Everyone is deprived of one thing or another. You aren't the only one without a big TV, cute clothes, rich parents, or a nice car. Today, learn to be happy with what you have, because if you are always wishing for something else, you will always feel deprived in life.

Clean Your Room

With the end of summer in sight, you are probably feeling good because you've had a couple of months to relax and play, but how is your bedroom holding up? Are there suntan lotion stains on your carpet, sand in your bed, magazines and water bottles cluttering your desk, or tank tops lying on your closet floor? Summertime can leave your room in need of some serious attention.

Cleaning your room may sound like a drag, but it's not. Turn on your favorite music as you fold your clothes, put your belongings away, get rid of cluttering junk, vacuum in corners, and dust your shelves. Clean the places that haven't been cleaned in years, like under your bed, and your closet, bookshelves, and desk. You will see that getting your space into top shape will clear your mind and get you ready to jump into the new school year.

Have a Clothing Swap

If you're anything like me, your closet is full of clothes that you haven't worn in years. Stuff you keep in hopes that "someday I'll wear that." Cleaning your room in order to get ready for the new school year means cleaning out everything, especially your closet.

This is the perfect time to arrange a clothing swap with your girlfriends. Ask all your friends to clean out their closets, then get together and trade all your old clothes and accessories. Tell everyone to bring shirts, pants, dresses, shoes, scarves, necklaces, or anything else that's been hiding deep in their closets. Maybe someone will have a shirt that goes perfectly with your favorite skirt, or one of your friends will fall in love with those funky pants your grandma gave you last Christmas. Give the clothes that are left over to younger siblings or charity.

A clothing swap is a great way to clean your closet and add new pieces to your wardrobe without spending a penny.

Rearrange Your Room

Rearranging your room is another fun activity to do before school starts. Get the feel of a whole new room simply by moving around your furniture and putting your belongings in new places. If my room is left the same way for too long, I feel like I'm in a rut. So when my life starts feeling dull, I move things around, and that livens me up.

Today, rearrange your room. Put your bed by the window, or push your bookshelves against a different wall. Move your stereo, and reorganize your books. Place your desk at an angle, and play with different ways of lighting by moving around your lamps.

Moving around your furniture is a free, easy way to remodel your room. The different arrangement will give you a fresh start on the year to come.

Create a Haven

Now that your room is spotless, you can turn it into your personal sanctuary. You need a place to retreat to for daydreaming, relaxing, painting your nails, studying, listening to music, or just being yourself.

Decorate your room so that even a perfect stranger could walk in and see your personality. Hang paintings on your walls, and fill your bulletin board with pictures of friends, postcards of places you've traveled to, or favorite quotes. Decorate your bedside table with framed pictures, a vase of flowers, or scented candles. Put comfortable blankets on your bed, find a neat lamp, and always keep your favorite books on the shelves.

Create a space that reflects you. When school starts, you will love escaping to your personal haven.

The Rule of Four Seasons

My nineteen-year-old friend Nick says that he needs to know a girl for a year before he knows what she's really like. "There are four seasons, and everyone acts differently during each one. You have to know a girl for a full year so that you can see how she changes with the seasons. That's about how long it takes me to see if I really like a girl."

You may think that a guy is perfect for you after a month, but you don't really know him yet. Use the rule of four seasons when dealing with guys, and remember that the great guy you met this summer could change his personality as soon as the leaves change in the fall.

I'm not saying you shouldn't like or date a guy unless you've known him a year, just be aware of the four different seasons. It takes about a year of knowing a guy, whether you are dating, just friends, or somewhere in between, before you know his true personality.

Inspiring Words for the Year Ahead

What do you want for the upcoming school year? Do you hope to be happy, get good grades, give to others, discover a hidden talent, or read a lot? Use these last summer days to find something that will provide you with inspiration during the coming year.

Go to the library, read books of poetry, or look up uplifting quotes on the Internet. Maybe you know a line from your favorite movie or book; maybe your grandmother once said something that stands out in your mind. Find things written about what you love, values you have, ideals you wish to uphold, or dreams you hope to make come true. You might find that another person has been able to describe the innermost feelings you've never been able to put into words.

Decorate your poems or quotes once you've found them. Paint the words on beautiful paper, or type them out using a fun font on your computer. Draw a picture or make a collage to go along with it, and then hang it someplace in your room. Seeing your favorite poems and sayings every day will remind you of what you value most in life.

Balancing Money, Responsibility, and Fun

My mother often says, "A successful life is one that has money management, responsibility management, and fun management." As your summer draws to an end, and the new responsibilities of school are added, it is the perfect time to start balancing these things.

In your journal today, write about how you plan to handle your responsibilities, money, and fun during the new school year. Responsibilities? Make a vow to study at least one hour every day, or get your chores done first thing when you come home from school. Money? Maybe you want to open a savings account and start saving a little bit of all the money you get over the next year to go toward college, a car when you turn sixteen, or a new stereo for your bedroom. Fun? Write out a plan for how you're going to make time for fun in your busy schedule.

It is much easier to enjoy responsibilities, money, and fun time when you find your perfect balance of the three.

Call an Old Friend

You're probably familiar with the saying, "Make new friends but keep the old. One is silver and the other's gold." It can be easy to lose touch with friends during the summer because you aren't seeing everyone at school every day. Today, call a friend you haven't talked to in a while, a friend who moved away, someone you've drifted apart from but have been missing lately, or even an acquaintance you haven't talked to in a while. Keep old friendships going because, as the rhyme says, old friends are priceless.

Why Can't I Stop Fighting with My Mom?

You have probably noticed that since you became a teen, you are having a harder time getting along with your mother. I'll bet you never thought it was possible to fight so much with someone. You don't like fighting with her, but you have a hard time stopping, and you may not even be exactly sure why the two of you have such a hard time getting along.

The struggle between a teenage girl and her mother is a universal one. You are pulling away, trying to separate and define your own personality, while your mother is struggling to keep you close. Having angry feelings toward your mother is normal, so don't feel guilty. These rocky times will not last forever. My girlfriends and I fought the most with our mothers during eighth and ninth grade, but by the time we were juniors in high school, fighting with our moms was a rare occurrence.

Go to Dad for Help

When fights with your mom escalate to a point where you feel out of control, enraged, or completely devastated, Dad is always a good guy to talk to. Because your dad knows your mom so well, he may be able to explain the reasons behind her actions. Having a discussion with him could shed a new light on the difficulties you are having with your mom.

Explain to your dad the frustrations you are feeling toward your mother. Give him your side of the story; tell him what you want and what you wish your mother would do differently. Get his advice and find out what he observes as a third party. Ask him if he would be willing to talk to your mom and explain your point of view to her, or if he could be a mediator between you and your mom to help work out your disagreements. Dad can be the person who listens to your frustrations, helps you understand your mother, and is a neutral middleman who can help you and your mom work out your problems.

Rent an '80s Movie

Do you ever feel frustrated about being a teenage girl? Are you sick and tired of listening to gossip, being confused about guys, and riding in the front seat of an emotional roller coaster? There's a perfect cure for your feelings of teen frustration, and it's as close as the nearest video rental store.

Nothing understands or defines adolescent confusion like an '80s coming-of-age flick. Some of the classics are *Pretty in Pink*, *The Breakfast Club*, *Can't Buy Me Love*, *Sixteen Candles*, *Say Anything*, and *Ferris Bueller's Day Off*. These movies will crack you up (What were they thinking when they wore those clothes?), they'll leave you feeling excited about being a teen, and there's no doubt that you'll be able to relate to the characters.

Whether you watch them alone or with your girlfriends, '80s movies are bound to speak to you and leave you saying, "That's *exactly* what I'm going through."

Who's Your "Ordinary" Role Model?

We often look up to movie stars, professional athletes, models, musicians, and anyone else we see in the media. We admire what they do and want to be rich and well known like them. It's great to have famous role models, but it's also important to look up to "real" people, like parents, teachers, family, friends, and coaches. These are people who you see just about every day, people who know and care about you.

Today, look for your "ordinary" role model; somebody whose attitude about life you admire or who has accomplished something you hope to do someday. Choose someone you can go to for advice and look to for guidance.

Pick Your Clothes with Care

Every important memory I have of my life is made more vivid by what I was wearing. I can easily recall what I wore on the first day of school every year from seventh grade through my senior year of high school. I know what I was wearing when I was fourteen and my first true love kissed me for the first time, just as I remember the clothes I had on when he broke up with me a year and a half later. And I know everything I wore to every dance, even if I sometimes have trouble recalling who my date was. Just like Ilene Beckerman says in her book *Love, Loss, and What I Wore,* "I don't remember the boy I went with or the prom, just the dress."

Today, pick your clothes with care. Dress comfortably in what makes *you* feel pretty; your clothing will be part of what helps define important moments in your life. Even though you may forget who you were with or what they said, the memory of what you wore is bound to stick with you.

So You Want to Be Popular?

"What if nobody likes me and I don't have any friends?" I asked my mother nervously before my first day of junior high.

"Of course people will like you," she said, trying to encourage me.

"How do you know? I might end up being the biggest nerd in school!"

My mom smiled. "When I was in high school during the '60s, I read some advice from Ann Landers. I have never forgotten it, and it has never failed me. It was: If you want to be popular and have people like you, smile and say, 'Hi' to everyone you pass. *Everyone!*"

No matter how old, this advice is still worth hearing. Being popular is often as simple as a smile. Everyone likes a person who smiles. It may be hard when you are feeling shy or intimidated, but the more you force yourself to smile at everyone you see, the sooner it will become the natural thing for you to do.

Soul Food

If you ate nothing but french fries, chocolate, pop-corn, and soda pop, your body would feel sick and completely unhealthy. Imagine how lazy your brain would feel and how unintelligent you would be if you never read a book, never did homework, and never challenged yourself to think hard. Most of us pay attention to the needs of our minds and bodies, so why is it that we so often feed our souls nothing but junk?

What things make your soul feel terrible? My version of soul-junk is watching violence on television or listening to people make hateful comments about others. Today, think about your types of soul-junk and do something to nourish your soul. Meditate by sitting quietly in your room with candles lit, or by sitting outside in your favorite nature setting. Go to church, write in your journal, go for a bike ride in the park, or look at the stars. These things are soul food that will help to keep your soul feeling healthy.

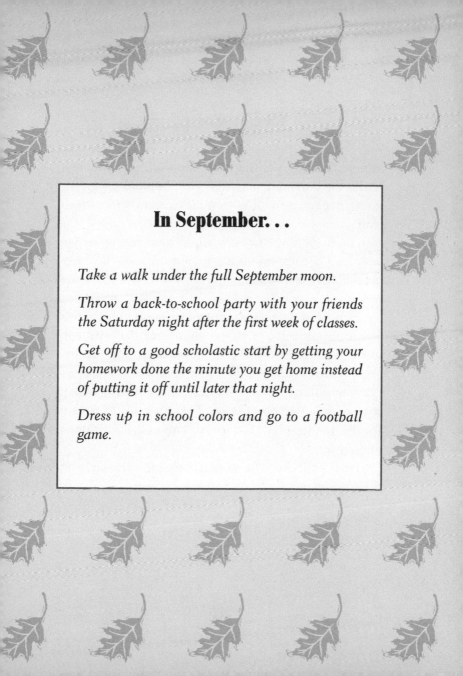

In September. . .

Take a walk under the full September moon.

Throw a back-to-school party with your friends the Saturday night after the first week of classes.

Get off to a good scholastic start by getting your homework done the minute you get home instead of putting it off until later that night.

Dress up in school colors and go to a football game.

A Fresh Start

When you are a student, September, not January, marks the beginning of a new year. September means going back to school with a clean slate and a fresh start.

The beginning of a new school year can be nerve-wracking because of all the uncertainty—will I have good classes, will I make friends, will I have the same lunchtime as my friends?

Today, forget about the unknowns and think of this as an opportunity to shape your year the way you want. What do you want to do this year? You can get good grades because right now you have an A in every class, or you can make new friends by having lunch with people you don't know. Do you want to try out for the school play? Go for it! The cast hasn't been chosen yet.

This is the beginning of a new school year, and there are many exciting adventures ahead of you!

Help Out the Younger Girls

The typical cycle found in schools is that the older girls always hate the girls in grades beneath them. I think it's because the older girls are a little worried about the new girls. My friends and I always wondered, "Will the younger girls steal all our guys?"

Before you start picking on the younger girls, think about when you were in their position. Remember how much you looked up to the older girls, how mature they seemed, and how badly you hoped they would like you. Now that you have thought about those feelings, cut the younger girls some slack. Instead of being a bully, be their role model. Help them out and say hello. Today, remember that there's no reason to be mean to somebody just because they are younger than you.

The New Girl

"We're moving." Your parents sprung the news on you, and now you're the new girl at school. It's hardest to switch schools during the teenage years, and it takes a lot of courage to go to a school where you don't know a single person. Classes, breaks, lunches, and weekends may be lonely for a while, because it may seem nearly impossible to break into already formed friendship circles. You will miss your friends from home and may even initially dislike all the people you meet at your new school.

Try not to bask in the self-pity and bitterness you feel about your move. The best thing you can do is get involved. Look for clubs that interest you, join a sports team, or volunteer to help decorate for the upcoming dance. If you put in a little effort, your "new" label will disappear, and you will fit perfectly into your new environment.

Write Yourself a Back-to-School Letter

At the beginning of every new school year, I get excited when I think about the year to come. Will my friends and I have fun together, or will we fight and grow apart? Am I going to make the volleyball team? Is this going to be the year that I meet the boy of my dreams?

Today, write yourself a letter to read in June, when school is finished. Go someplace you love—your nature spot, your favorite coffee shop, or your own room. Write about your life now. Who are your friends? What classes are you taking? Let your imagination go, and write about what you hope for in the year to come. Do you want to learn to play the guitar or meet some new people? Maybe you hope to overcome your shyness and try out for cheerleading. Where will you be in June?

When you have finished, seal the letter and put it on your bulletin board, or tuck it in your diary. During the last week of school, take it out and read it. It will be fun to see how your life has changed.

Put Effort into Making Friends

A friend once said to me, "You make friends so easily." This was a complete shock to me. I never thought of my friendships as something come by easily. I worked hard at them. Everything during my teens revolved around my friendships. I would invite people over to my house, make a point to talk to them during breaks, and call them just to say hi. The only reason I ever joined Honor Society and played sports was to meet people.

Making and keeping friends is work. Some people have just learned the skill of friendship more quickly and work harder at it than others. If you have a deep desire to be friends with the girl who sits in front of you in math class or the guy who has the locker below yours, you must make the effort. Go out of your way to say hello. Sit with her at lunch. Ask him what he is doing for the weekend. Invite her to go to the football game on Friday with you. People feel good when others show an interest in them. You don't have to be overbearing, just show that you are willing to become friends.

Who Wants Yellow Teeth?

If somebody offered you a glass of a liquid that would give you a good feeling for a while, would you drink it even if it had an awful color and stench? What if you knew that if you continued to drink it, you would become addicted and would suffer health problems. Would you sacrifice your health for the good feeling the drink gave you? Would you take a sip if the drink was poison and could kill you?

Nobody in their right mind would deliberately hurt themselves—or would they? The sad truth is that thousands of teens harm themselves in this way every day by smoking cigarettes.

Everybody knows the negative effects of smoking, so why do teens choose to do it? Smoking turns your teeth yellow, gives you bad breath, and makes your hair and clothes stink. Not only is it totally unattractive, it also fills your lungs with black smoke and tar, makes it hard for you to breathe, gives you a terrible cough, and causes many diseases such as emphysema and lung cancer. Smoking also harms everyone around you. So, if you are thinking of starting this habit, you may want to think again.

My Parents Are So Embarrassing

Your mom wears weird clothes and talks loudly in public, and your dad insists on giving the third degree to every boy that sets foot into your house. You wish you could wear a sheet over your head when you are with your parents. You feel like everyone is watching you and thinking, "What a dork she must be if she's with parents who act like *that!*" You often wonder why you got stuck with such humiliating parents.

Everyone thinks his or her parents aren't normal. All parents have some crazy quirk that gets on your nerves and embarrasses you to no end. Your parents are human, they aren't perfect, and they will never be perfect no matter how hard you try and make them be. So today, give them a break. Try not to roll your eyes, sigh, or say, "Mother, would you quit doing that?" Just let your parents be themselves. Remember that their "embarrassing" behavior is noticeable only to you. I guarantee you that nobody notices your parent's quirks like you do. You may even start to enjoy your parents' quirks and be amused by them instead of annoyed.

I'm Different from You and That's Great

Most people think of diversity as many people of different races, but diversity goes far beyond skin color. Diversity simply means variety. Think of the variety of people at your school. Some are interested in math, some are into art, some like writing, and others enjoy wood shop. There are kids who are Muslim, Jehovah's Witness, Mormon, Buddhist, and Jewish, while other students don't believe in religion at all. Some like golf, some like football, and some like to fish.

Diversity is the spice of life! The world would be pretty boring if everyone was the same! You are different, even different from your closest friends, and that's okay. Today, acknowledge the diversity that surrounds you and accept people who have different interests and beliefs than yours.

Overcoming Jealousy

I grew up in an upper-class town, but for my family, money was tight. My friends shopped at places like Banana Republic and Abercrombie, while I searched for name-brand bargains at a discount store and then lied and said I only shopped at Nordstrom. When a friend would come to school in a new outfit, jealousy filled my heart. "Why do you always get new clothes?" I would ask, not even attempting to hide my bitterness. Everyone around me always looked so stylish, but I always felt clumsily put-together.

I got so sick of feeling jealous that my sophomore year I decided to get a job at the Gap. Not only could I earn money, but I also could get a discount on clothes. It was a perfect arrangement.

It is natural for you to be jealous of your friends when they have more than you. Let yourself feel jealous, but don't let it fester inside of you. Use your jealousy as a motivation for doing something positive for yourself instead of just complaining or feeling bitter.

Learn the Joys of Learning

What do you get out of school? Why are you there? If someone asked me that when I was thirteen, I would have said I was there for my friends or because I didn't have a choice. By my senior year, I discovered that I was at school to learn.

Learning isn't about turning in your homework on time, acing your German final, graduating with straight A's, or getting into Harvard. Somebody could do these things without learning anything. Learning means engaging your mind and becoming excited about the new knowledge you are gaining. It's about loving the book you read in English class so much that you read another book by the same author just for fun, or about being so excited about your science project that you stay home on a Friday night to work on it.

Today, instead of just jumping through the hoops for a good grade, be open to learning. Listen closely to your teacher's lecture, read your assignments carefully, and devote time to the subjects you enjoy. Make learning come to life. You will get more than you could ever imagine out of school if you discover the joy of learning.

Shooting for Popularity

The two most popular girls in my seventh grade were Jayme and Michelle. One was tall with long blonde hair and looked fifteen, and the other was short with brown hair, tan skin, and an adorable smile. They walked around campus with an entourage of boys, and you just had to be seen talking to one of them to be boosted up the social ladder.

I longed to be one of those girls. I tried to imagine what kinds of things they liked to do after school, what they talked about, and what types of people they liked. Hoping, praying, and wishing that I could be popular, I would have done anything to be their friend. Popularity is like a stamp of approval saying you're a good person. Since everyone liked Michelle and Jayme, I thought I needed to be like them in order to have people like me.

Popularity isn't the route to happiness. The popular people are always changing; those popular in seventh grade might not be popular in eighth grade or high school. Are you willing to risk losing your true identity to be popular? Playing the popularity game is a gamble everyone loses in the end.

Judging by the Insides

Since kindergarten, we've been told stories like "The Ugly Duckling" and "The Frog Prince" that reinforce the truth that looks are only temporary and inner character is what defines a great person.

If we know these lessons, why do we continually place such a high value on appearances? Prettiness doesn't equal happiness. There are many "pretty" girls who are mean and hate their lives and many "ugly" girls who are extremely nice and love life.

Your looks are just your packaging, the housing where your spirit, heart, and brain live. It's time for us to start putting the "It's what's on the inside" motto into practice.

Today, practice one way of following the motto. Stop judging others by their looks. A person's sense of humor, caring heart, honesty, or fun-loving spirit aren't characteristics you can see just by looking. Lift up yourself and others by refraining from comments like, "She looks terrible in that outfit," or, "Why doesn't she do something to make her hair look better?" Jump off the critical comments bandwagon.

Flaunt It—
Your Personality, That Is

Here is another way of putting the "It's what's on the inside" motto into practice. Stop putting so much emphasis on your own looks. Think about how much time you spend doing your hair, picking out your clothes, and putting on makeup.

Today, take fifteen minutes to think about how you're going to let your wonderful inner qualities shine. How can you show others your generosity, intelligence, enthusiasm, and joy? Instead of worrying about how you're going to make your body look good, think about how you're going to flaunt your sparkling personality. The more you focus on your personality, the more others will see the beautiful girl you are on the inside.

A Step above Ordinary

According to Webster's dictionary, the definition of the word *extraordinary* is "going far beyond the ordinary; unusual; remarkable." Does this definition apply to your life? Do you live in an extraordinary way, or would the definition for *usual* (custom; common; the most often seen, used, and done) fit your life better?

Many times we are so afraid to be labeled as weird that we don't dare do anything that goes against the common, everyday norms of our peers. The ordinary way of living is about getting by, making do with life, blending in, and taking the safe route. It's about getting your homework done without really learning; only sitting with people you know instead of meeting someone new; or having a conversation with your mother without really listening.

Be extraordinary today! Follow your own rhythm to beyond usual because life is too important for us to merely get by.

I'm So Shy!

"I hate how shy I am," I said to my friend, Amy, who promptly disagreed with me.

"Amanda," she said, "you are not shy."

"Yes I am!" I argued. "Whenever I'm with a group of people, I feel uncomfortable, and I have a hard time talking to people unless I know them well. I don't say much in class, and I can't introduce myself to strangers at parties."

Everyone feels shy sometimes. It's natural to feel uncomfortable when you are in new situations. The difference between those who are shy and those who aren't is the way they handle their uncomfortable feelings.

You can do many things to overcome shyness. Imagine that everyone is feeling as shy as you are, and when you walk down the halls at school, smile at people even if you don't know them. Not only does it make you feel more confident, it will help others feel more comfortable around you. Once you have established a "smiling relationship" with people, it makes it much easier to introduce yourself or strike up a conversation when you see them in class or at a party.

Lovin' the Single Life

Whenever my family gets together, one of my relatives' first questions is, "Do you have a boyfriend?" During the times I didn't (which was often), I would watch the disappointment on their faces as I said, "No, I'm single." I always felt I had to come up with some explanation like, "There aren't any guys worth dating at my school," or, "I'm too busy right now."

We girls are constantly given the impression that we won't be complete until we have a boyfriend. We spend crazy amounts of time looking for a guy. We categorize every male we know by whether he is boyfriend material or "just friendship" material. We read magazine articles entitled, "Fifty Ways to Make the Guy of Your Dreams Go Crazy over You!" We look at other couples and feel depressed because we don't have a boyfriend. "What's wrong with me?" single girls often wonder.

Nothing! Stop believing the old myth that having a boyfriend makes you better. In fact, the opposite is true. The sign of a strong, healthy girl is one who doesn't feel incomplete without a guy. Enjoy your single time, develop your interests, and get to know yourself.

If Life Is a Movie, Be the Star

In his poem "The Lady of Shalott," Alfred, Lord Tennyson tells the story of a lady who sits weaving in her room all day long. Afraid to join the world, she sits in front of a mirror that reflects the world she is not part of. She watches streams flow, birds sing, groups of girls wandering down the road laughing together, knights riding by on horses, and lovers walking together hand in hand. Having withdrawn from the world, the Lady of Shalott doesn't know what it's like to experience the feelings that go along with life.

Have you ever let your fear of failure become so big that you've stopped yourself from joining in on life? Instead of trying out for the basketball team, you sit on the sidelines and watch. You drop out of the school play auditions because you're afraid you won't get the lead role. Success and failure are so inter-twined in life that in order to experience one, you will inevitably experience the other.

Today, instead of watching life like an audience member at a movie, play the leading role. Dive in and be the star. If you're too afraid of failure, you'll never allow yourself to succeed.

Connect with Your Friends

Have you ever felt left out, or like you just don't fit in and nobody seems to care about having you around or hearing what you have to say? I have felt this way many times, sometimes while standing around with a group of people at a party. I try to join in the conversation by saying something like, "Oh yeah, I heard about that," but nobody takes notice of me.

If you find that hanging out with your friends means that you are constantly being left out, made fun of, or misunderstood, maybe it's time to find some new friends. Expand your friendship circle and look for people who want you to be a part of their lives. You deserve to have friends who are excited to see you and who make you feel that they like having you around. It's more rewarding to have a few friends who make you feel accepted than to have a ton of friends who don't care much at all.

Wasting Your Dancing Shoes on Boys Who Don't Dance

It was my first junior high dance. I spent hours getting ready because I'd heard stories about perfect strangers falling in love after dancing one slow song. Derek, the boy of my dreams, was going to be there, and I wanted to make myself beautiful so he'd fall for me.

When the first slow song came on, I turned Jeff down, hoping that Derek would ask me. Jordan, Brian, Paul, and Travis also asked. I turned them all down and sulked against the wall, waiting for my dream boy. When the DJ announced the last slow song, I mustered up all my courage, headed straight for Derek, and asked him dance, only to hear him say, "No, I hurt my ankle last night playing basketball." When I turned around for one last look, I saw Derek and his "hurt ankle" dancing with another girl.

Are you putting all your energy into a guy who never returns your affection? Stop wasting your time. You're passing up the opportunity to get to know other guys who find you beautiful, smart, and fun, and who will treat you nicely. Today, vow to put your energy into guys who return the effort.

Dealing with Teachers

Everyone is different when it comes to relating to teachers. Some girls can talk easily with teachers, some get nervous and feel shy around them, and others will say anything to make their teachers happy. Since you'll be around teachers for a long time, learning how to deal with them is a necessary survival skill.

Find out what your teachers expect and give it to them. If you show your teachers respect by paying attention in class, turning in your homework on time, and using common politeness, most teachers will give you the same respect back.

Not the Teacher's Pet

In a perfect world, all teachers would be fair all of the time. However, teachers are human—they play favorites, make mistakes, and can judge students incorrectly.

If you feel you've been treated unfairly by your teacher, confront him or her. Take some time to think out what you will say. Don't just whine or say, "I think you are mean to me." Give specific examples like, "I felt like you were picking on me last Monday when you made a joke about how I didn't understand the math problem." Ask your teacher if you could schedule some time to meet. Be calm and mature, and if your teacher continues to treat you unfairly, seek help from your parents and talk to a school counselor or the principal.

It's hard to confront a teacher, but once you get the courage to act and get your problem cleared up, you will be able to enjoy class much more. Remember, you should always feel comfortable and respected when you are in the classroom.

An Explosion of Emotion

"Why am I so emotional?" I wondered, frustrated by my ever-changing feelings. One day I would be totally happy and excited about life, and the next, I would feel depressed and worried for no apparent reason. "I wish I could just do away with all of my crazy emotions and just be a normal person!"

Teenage girls are full of emotion. Every day, you are growing up, facing challenges, having "first" experiences, and learning new things about life. Your hormones are racing, which also messes around with your emotions. Since teenage years tend to be an explosion of new things, it's only natural that you will also have an explosion of feelings. You may be frustrated with your emotions, but don't forget to enjoy them as well. My emotions have evened out now that I'm twenty, and I often find myself longing for the days when spine-tingling excitement would fill me before a school dance, or I felt complete happiness when hanging out at a party with my friends.

Today, be patient with your emotions and remember that they will not always be so extreme.

Catch a Clue

My mother and I got up at six o'clock in the morning on my sixteenth birthday so I could get my driver's license. We drove to the DMV, stood in line, and waited so I could take the test. I pictured driving my friends, music blasting, to the football games. Things didn't work out; I failed both my written and driving test and didn't get my license until a few weeks later.

I was relieved once I got my license, thinking I had encountered all my driving trauma. Little did I know they were just beginning. Within the first two years of driving, I got two speeding tickets, had five small fender-benders, and totaled two cars.

Pay attention to the signs you encounter in life. Lose the friend who tells white lies before she majorly betrays you. Start studying harder for math when you get a D on the first quiz, because it'll be too late when you fail the final. Catch the clues before they mess up your life in a bigger way. If I'd learned after failing my driver's test that I had to pay attention when I drove, I'd have spared myself a great deal of pain, and money.

Swim for Your Life

Life is like swimming in the ocean. Some days, the water is calm, and you swim with ease among the brightly colored fish, play with the dolphins, and admire the peaceful blue surroundings. You are comfortable trying out different strokes; you even swim on your back or your side. You dive in, hold your breath, twirl underwater, and pop up again. Yet overnight, drastic changes can take place. The sky fills with clouds and throws heavy rain against your face, monstrous waves hold you underwater as you struggle to get up, and sharks circle you, charting out their attack.

As poet Carl Sandburg once said, in order to stay afloat in the rough waters of life, you must keep swimming. Many times storms will hit without warning. When your friends betray you, or you become overloaded with homework, wreck your car, get dumped, or fail a class, you may feel like you're at the bottom of the ocean, scrambling to catch your breath. Sometimes there is nothing you can do but stay afloat and wait for the storm to pass.

I'm Leaving This Place Better Than I Found It

You are part of a community that is dependent upon all the people within it. What have you done for your community lately? Not much, huh? You don't think you have time for volunteer work or becoming involved in a community organization, do you?

Helping your community doesn't take a lot of time, and it's an extremely important action. Volunteerism isn't just about doing a big community service project; it can be something as small as picking up a piece of garbage off the ground.

Today, whenever you leave a place, leave it a little bit better than you found it. If you go into a classroom where the desks are all out of order, put them back where you know they belong, or if you are at the library, pick up the trash from around the table you're working at, even if you didn't make it. Whether it's for your school, neighborhood, or town, contribute to your community.

Stop Fighting with Armies

You and Caleigh aren't on speaking terms. At lunch, you sit at a table telling Melanie, Krista, Erik, and Gavin what a terrible friend Caleigh is, while she stands in the bathroom telling Shelly, Heather, and Marci that you are a backstabber.

When we girls are in fights, we build up armies against each other. In your irrational frenzy, you forget that having more people on your "side" doesn't mean that you have won; in fact, you may be hurting your cause more than helping. You will only hurt your "neutral" friends if you force them to choose sides. They have nothing to do with your fight, so it's best if you allow them to stay out of it.

Express your feelings and straighten out the mess by discussing it only with close friends, preferably ones who aren't close to the friend you are fighting with. If you are in a fight with a friend, the best thing to do is keep it to yourself and resist the temptation to get everyone else involved, too.

Fun for the Whole Family?

"Why don't you ever want to go to the movies with me?" my mom would ask.

"It's just not the same," I would say.

"We can go to whatever movie you want to, so you'll have just as much fun as you do with your friends," she'd reply.

What my mom didn't understand was that with my friends, the movie we actually saw was irrelevant to the amount of fun we had. Getting dressed up, joking around while waiting in line for tickets, looking for cute boys to sit in front of in the theater, hoping the cute boys ask for your number after the movie—that's what going to the movies with friends is all about.

You just can't do these kinds of things with the family. As Jerry Seinfeld so wisely put it, "There is no such thing as fun for the whole family." Friends are nice, but spending time with your parents and siblings is also important. Just because your family isn't as much fun as your friends doesn't mean that they can't be fun—it's just a different kind of fun.

Do a Little Dance

School dances when nobody brought a date and everyone danced with whomever they wanted was one of my favorite things about junior high. I was so nervous during the first dance I went to that I said, "I don't know how to dance!" So instead of dancing all night with everyone, I stood in the back talking to friends and drinking punch, only joining in when a guy would ask me to slow dance.

Standing on the sidelines is never any fun. Grab a group of girlfriends and get down! Don't worry about looking stupid; everyone's too busy having fun themselves to worry about what you look like.

If you know a dance is coming up and you are feeling nervous about dancing, follow Madonna's advice and practice in your room where nobody can see you. This way you can become comfortable dancing before you show your moves to the whole school. When the next dance comes along, you'll be the first one to jump in and start dancing.

Drink Smart—Or Not at All

Perhaps curiosity has gotten the better of you, and you have decided that you want to drink. Whether this is your first time experimenting with alcohol or you've done it many times, there is one rule that always applies when alcohol is involved: BE CAREFUL!

Drinking alcohol makes you less inhibited, and you will most likely do something you wouldn't do if you were sober. Maybe you'll spill a secret you promised not to say a word about, or call the ex-boyfriend you swore never to call again because you're trying desperately to get over him, or get together with a guy you barely know, or get into a car with someone who has been drinking. I have done and said things when I was "buzzed" that I kicked myself for in the morning.

Keep control of yourself when drinking and don't go over your limit. Here's a clue: If you puke, you've had *way* too much to drink. The best decision is not to drink at all—you will be much happier, both physically and emotionally. If you are going to use alcohol, do it in moderation.

I Just Met the Boy
I'm Gonna Marry

There's a new guy in your life. He's cute, funny, and easy to talk to, and the two of you have a great time together. You dream about what it will be like when you have been dating for a year, and you scribble your first name with his last name attached. But when your best friend asks you, "What's Jake's middle name?" you pause for a minute and say, "I don't know. We've only been together two weeks."

It's definitely time for you to slow down! Not every guy you date will be your dream guy, and not every relationship you have has to be a serious one. Not all relationships get progressively more intense over time—some stay simple. I call these "Just-for-Fun Relationships." You both enjoy hanging out together, but you both know that nothing serious is going to develop.

Meeting a guy you have fun with is a great feeling, but it doesn't mean that he's your soul mate. Some relationships will grow, while others will stay the same. Don't complicate your relationship by worrying if the two of you will still be together three months from now. Relax and just have a good time!

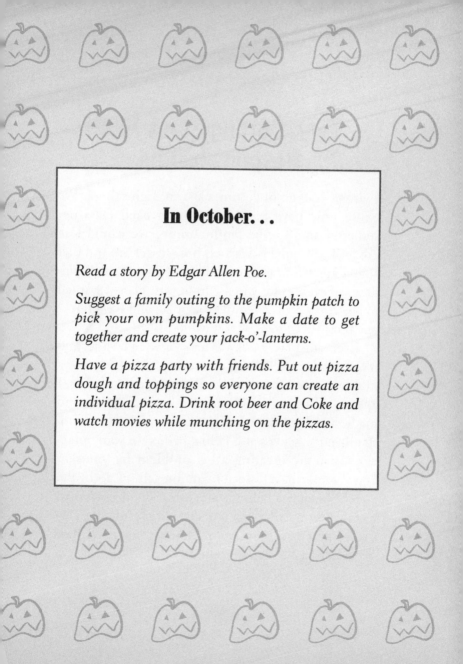

In October. . .

Read a story by Edgar Allen Poe.

Suggest a family outing to the pumpkin patch to pick your own pumpkins. Make a date to get together and create your jack-o'-lanterns.

Have a pizza party with friends. Put out pizza dough and toppings so everyone can create an individual pizza. Drink root beer and Coke and watch movies while munching on the pizzas.

Even Cutting Class Has Responsibilities

I was the queen of cutting class in high school. We could only have nine absences in each class per semester, and on the tenth absence we would lose credit, but I quickly learned how to get around that rule. I knew how to sweet-talk teachers and had hundreds of excuses for why I had to miss class. I wanted to be on my own schedule, socialize, and have fun—anything but sit in class and work.

Everyone plays hooky at least once in awhile, and it's perfectly okay as long as you don't let it become a problem. Even though I missed quite a bit of class, I always called a friend to get the assignments and made sure I got the work in on time. If you are constantly missing class and falling behind in your homework, you are creating a big problem for yourself. You'll either have a lot of catching up to do in the end, or you'll risk failing your class. Skipping class can be tons of fun and a much-needed break from the regular routine of school, but remember that even playing hooky has its responsibilities.

Say Good-bye to Cliques

It's great to have close friends—girls you can tell all your secrets to, share bonding times with, and lean on when you need help. Sometimes groups of girls can turn from friends into cliques, those girls who travel in packs and snub those who aren't "in."

While tight friendships are important, it's also important to have a wide variety of friends. Don't put all your time and energy into just one group. The older you become, the more you'll find that you need different types of people in your life. Be open to people other than your best friends. You may discover that the girl who sits across from you in painting class shares your love of art museums, while your best friends think museums are completely boring.

You have many talents and interests. Don't neglect these interests by hanging out with one group of people who fill only one part of your life.

Phenomenal Woman— That's You

I wanted to be the beautiful girl of the school, the one whom guys flocked to, dreamed about, and got tongue-tied over. I wished for slender legs, long and shiny hair, clear skin, and bright eyes. I wanted to make guys look twice when I walked down the street, or forget their meals when I entered the restaurant.

When I read Maya Angelou's poem "Phenomenal Woman," my desires changed. Instead of wanting to be outwardly pretty, I wanted people to notice my beautiful soul. Maya Angelou's poem is about a woman who drew people to her because of her personality, not her looks. Even though she wasn't beautiful on the outside, she was beautiful on the inside.

Today, read Maya Angelou's poem and be your own Phenomenal Woman. We may not be able to change the looks we're born with, but we do have complete control over our inner beauty. Celebrate your warmth, passion, excitement, caring, joy, gratitude, and strength—everything that is beautiful about the you inside.

Flex Your Courage Muscle

When you hear the word *courage*, what images come to mind? Do you picture Martin Luther King, Jr., giving his "I Have a Dream" speech or Rosa Parks refusing to move to the back of the bus? Do you imagine Amelia Earhart, the first woman to fly around the world? How about Peace Corps workers helping children in Africa or firefighters rushing into a burning house to save a family?

You possess just as much courage as the bravest person in the world. Being courageous doesn't always mean taking a stand for human rights or risking your life for another's. Courage is as simple as standing up for a friend when you hear people saying mean things about her, admitting when you have done something wrong, or even refusing to get into a car with a driver who has been drinking. Courage is about doing what you believe is right, even if it means going against the crowd or making others mad at you.

Today, be brave! Courage is like a muscle, and if you don't use it, it will wither. Exercise your courage regularly, and you will become as strong and brave as the people you admire.

I Wanna Look Like a Model

The one thing that drives me absolutely crazy is listening to guys talk about models. "Those girls aren't real!" I say, irritated after hearing guys oohh and ahh over some "chick" they saw on MTV last night. "And you wonder why girls have eating disorders and low self-esteem?"

"You girls shouldn't be so sensitive about it," argues one guy.

Guys just don't get it. They don't experience the same self-image pressures we do. Every day, girls are slammed with images of the "ideal" girl we are supposed to live up to. Think of what she's done to reach her perfection—hours of getting her hair and makeup done, a fashion team to pick out her outfit, a computer to "fix" her imperfections, and possibly even plastic surgery. It's ridiculous! If you had a crew following you around and fixing your hair or reapplying your makeup every ten minutes, you would look perfect too.

The media gives us completely distorted images of girls. Don't try to live up to these unattainable standards, and don't feel bad about yourself when you don't look like the cover model for *Seventeen*. You are a real girl with natural beauty.

Drama Queen

"Fine!!!" Brandy yelled. She threw her sandwich against the lunch table and stomped out of the cafeteria in a huff, tears streaming from her eyes.

"There she goes again," one person said, as we all laughed at the scene our friend just made. "It's impossible to take her seriously when she makes everything into such a drama!"

We all play the Drama Queen now and then—those times when you exaggerate a story for sympathy, or talk about your terrible day in a voice loud enough that your entire class can hear. A soap opera life can get out of control if you don't watch out. Think carefully before you make a scene, and remember, there is a time and a place for everything. The cafeteria at lunch or the middle of a crowded hallway is not the best place for confronting someone who has been talking behind your back, or for getting into a screaming match with your boyfriend. Not only will these kinds of spectacles draw negative attention to you, it can make the people around you feel uncomfortable because now they're involved in something that isn't their business.

First Impressions

I was angry when my biology teacher assigned our lab partners and I got stuck with Melissa. I had heard some bad things about her, and although I didn't know her very well, she seemed like a snob, and I didn't like her. To my surprise, after a few weeks of working together, I realized that we had a lot in common, and we became friends.

Has this ever happened to you? You make a judgment about someone before you get to know them, and then later you realize your judgment was completely wrong? Our first impressions of people can often be incorrect. Be wary of making judgments about people when they are only based on what you've heard from others, who their friends are, or what you think they'd be like as a friend. Get to know people before you decide how you feel about them.

I had a friend in high school who once said, "I never make assumptions about people too early, because I have learned that my first impression is always wrong." Take this advice into account before you make that snap judgment.

Put "Have-to's" Before "Want-to's"

It's a warm fall afternoon, and your friends are going out for ice cream and then hitting the mall. You want to go, but something's holding you back—a history paper you haven't started yet and the math assignment that is due tomorrow. You, of course, want to be with your friends, so you try to convince yourself, "I'll get it done tonight. It won't be hard."

Before you ditch your homework, think for a moment. Are you going to spend the whole time thinking about what you have to do when you get home instead of enjoying the moment you're in? Relaxing is difficult when you have work to do because your mind is focused on your responsibilities, not the fun you are trying to have.

When procrastination tempts you, remember that you will enjoy yourself much better if you get your "have-to's" done before you dive into your "want-to's."

A Girl's Life Is a Country Song

I used to despise country music. Its twangy sound and depressing lyrics got on my nerves so much that I declared that no country music would be played on any of my radios. Then I went to college and learned an important lesson: A girl's life is a country song.

Country music speaks to a girl's heart like no other music can. With titles like "Did I Shave My Legs for This?" "She's in Love with the Boy," "Tonight the Heartache's on Me," or "Man! I Fell Like a Woman," female country singers show that they know our hearts, dreams, pains, struggles, and fears.

The next time you are feeling love-struck or lost in love, reach for Reba, Shania, the Dixie Chicks, or Trisha Yearwood. Nothing will capture your feelings, heal your hurts, or make you feel proud to be a girl like a good dose of female country music.

There's Plenty of Room for Victorious Girls in the World

I believed my best friend in junior high and high school was perfect. She was beautiful, smart, funny, and everyone loved her. Everything I did, she did better. Instead of feeling happy for her when she was elected Homecoming Queen, or when the boy she had a crush on asked her out, my heart filled with envy.

Watching her get recognized while I struggled clumsily along broke my heart. During my senior year of high school, though, I started finding things I was good at. Once I discovered I had great abilities, I stopped being jealous and was genuinely pleased by Sarah's success.

If you find yourself feeling resentful of a successful friend, ask yourself why. Are you jealous of the attention she's getting? Maybe you haven't yet found your own strengths, but your friends' accomplishments don't make you a failure. There's plenty of room for triumphant girls in this world—you are one of them! When a friend does something well, be happy for her, and know that your success is right around the corner.

I'm Gonna Scream

It's one of those days when I'm plain mad. Mad at Mom, mad at school, mad at the dog, mad at life. My teeth are clenched and my fists are tight. I'm brewing with anger, and if someone says the wrong thing to me, I just might snap.

Do you ever feel like a volcano is trapped inside you, and the longer you keep it bottled up, the stronger it will become? Let it out! That's right, go somewhere by yourself and erupt like a can of soda that has been shaken up and explodes on opening. Sprint fast and hard around a track, yell as loudly as you can in the middle of a field, or blast your music and sing at the top of your lungs.

Get rid of your anger before you take it out on an innocent bystander like your best friend, your little brother, or your grandma. You don't want to say or do something you'll regret once your mad spell has passed. Most important, don't let your anger brew inside and make you bitter at the world. Stomp, yell, or throw something (*away* from other people) until every drop of anger has left you.

Give That Back!

You finally let your friend borrow your favorite black sweater, after weeks of pleading. You didn't want to, but she wanted to look good to get Austin's attention, and she promised to be careful with it. Now, two weeks later, she still hasn't returned it.

Maybe you've asked her about it, and she said she'd bring it to school but hasn't yet. Maybe you're a little nervous about asking for it back. Even something as small as a borrowed sweater, book, or money can cause a big rift in your friendship. If you've given your friend enough time to return what she's borrowed, it's time to ask for it back. If she still forgets, ask one of your parents to drive you to her house, and then call her up and say, "My dad and I are going to run some errands, so I thought I'd stop by and pick up the skirt you borrowed."

Next time a friend wants to borrow something you don't feel like lending out, feel free to say no. Remember, you can always use the good old excuse, "Sorry, but my mom got mad at me last time I let someone borrow my clothes."

Be Aware of Violence...

Violence is a constant part of our society, but we have become so desensitized that it rarely upsets us anymore. We listen to guys tell stories of the fights they got into and how they "kicked the other guy's ass." We don't blink an eye as we watch people get assaulted, stabbed, and shot in movies, and we aren't surprised when we hear about teens killing each other in schools.

Today, pay attention to the violence around you— how many times do you hear about, see it, and participate in it? Remember, violence doesn't always have to be physical, it can be as simple as saying something cruel about another person. The first step to putting an end to violence is becoming aware of it in the world around you.

. . .Now Stop It

You may wonder, "What can I do to end violence? Just one person can't make a difference." You can if you remember this: There are two options for everything you can do in life. The right path is the higher one and leads to love, peace, and happiness, while the wrong path leads only to violence and destruction.

Today, choose the right path. Refuse to listen to, watch, and participate in any form of violence. Nobody is born violent; we learn it from family, friends, and media. Take a stand against violence and let your actions teach others how to choose the right path as well.

Getting Ready for Halloween

Halloween is coming in two weeks, but have you thought about your costume? You are never too old to dress up, and Halloween is the perfect time to let your childhood spirit free. Start planning a fun Halloween event, like a costume party where everyone comes dressed up. Bob for apples, light jack-o'-lanterns, put up cobwebs, and have a prize for the best costume. Or get a group together for trick-or-treating and set a theme for your costumes; go as disco queens, mobsters, a group of different fruits, or a group of your favorite movie or storybook characters. Wear your costumes to school, and pass out candy to everyone.

Halloween is the perfect time to be something you've always wanted to be. The possibilities are endless, so go crazy this Halloween!

Why Am I Doing This?

I was involved in many things—student government, Honor Society, cheerleading, and the school newspaper. I did everything I was told would make me a well-rounded person and get me into a good college. None of these things ever left me feeling fulfilled. Nobody ever acknowledged my hard work or gave me praise for all I was doing.

By my senior year of high school, I was completely burned out. I looked at my pom-poms and my academic achievement awards and thought, "There must be more to life than this." I realized I had done it all for the wrong reasons. I wanted recognition and praise.

Find things that make you truly happy, not things you do for the reaction of others when they see what you have done. Paint a picture because you like to paint, not because you want somebody to tell you that you are a great artist, or join the dance team for your love of dance, not because it's what all the popular girls do.

Life is not about how much you do or how much others notice you; what's important is how you feel when you are doing it.

You're Right

When my mother and I argued, she would get frustrated with me and say, "You always have to have the last word in arguments. You're not always right."

"Neither are you," I would yell, and our argument would continue, sometimes for days. By the end, we had forgotten what we had begun fighting about, and our main concern was being right and proving the other wrong.

Don't fall into our rut. Make understanding, not winning, your main goal in arguments. When you say things like, "You're wrong," you invalidate the other person's feelings. You don't have to agree with their feelings, just be open to their point of view. Keep in mind that you both see the situation differently, so both of you are right.

Parents Who Drink

The first time I ever saw someone's parents drunk was at a party my sophomore year of high school. Not only were the parents allowing kids to drink in the house, but they were drinking right along with them. I was stunned as I watched these parents get drunk and act like children while their daughter ran around looking after them as if she were the adult.

If life always progressed the way it should, people would become more mature as they grew older. This doesn't always happen, and some adults act less mature than their children. If your parents have a drinking problem, know that it is not your responsibility. Nothing you have done has caused them to drink, and it isn't up to you to fix their problem.

To ease your own pain, frustration, and anger about your parents' drinking problem, you need to talk to somebody. Talk to a school or church counselor; they are there to help you with your problems, whatever they may be. These people can direct you and help you to deal with your feelings about your parents in a healthy way.

Down Times Will Be Bouncing Up Soon

You're feeling down in the dumps. Your life seems to be traveling from bad to worse at a rapid pace, and you wonder if things will get better. You may ask yourself, "Am I ever going to be happy again? Is the rest of my life going to be full of depression?"

No need to worry, things will get better—they always do. It's like playing with a bouncy ball; you throw the ball and it goes up high, but then it starts coming back down. It falls faster and faster until it hits the ground, and then it starts moving upward again. The ball can't go up again until it hits the ground.

Try to enjoy your down times and remember that the amount of unhappiness you are having in your life right now is a equivalent to the amount of happiness you can look forward to. Down times will start bouncing up sooner than you think!

We're Just Friends

Whenever I make a new guy friend or spend more time with one particular guy, my mom always asks, "Is he your boyfriend?" I always have to explain that we're just friends. "Just because I hang out with a guy doesn't mean we are dating," I always tell her.

Relationships between guys and girls have changed a lot since our moms were teens, which is why my mom had such a hard time understanding that most of the guys in my life were just friends. It's much more common for girls today to have friendships with guys.

When you have guy friends you can hang out with and talk to, you are able to learn about the opposite sex without having all the pressures of dating. Guy friends can be easier to get along with than girls because they tend to be less gossipy and emotional. Most boys are more loyal and won't stab you in the back the way girl friends can.

We are much luckier than our moms were. Being allowed to have boy *friends* can be much more fun than having a boyfriend.

I Forgive You

"I can't believe that Ryan and Jennifer are together!"

Shocked, I said, "They are not together."

"Yes, they are, Amanda," someone at the table corrected me.

I was furious! Ryan had been my boyfriend for a year, and we had just broken up. Jennifer had promised she would get us back together. How could they be dating? For the next few weeks, I told everyone they made a terrible couple and thought about how I could get back at them for betraying me.

One day I realized my anger was consuming me. If I wanted to move on with my life, I needed to forgive them. That night, I wrote in my journal, "I forgive Ryan for hurting me by getting together with someone else, and I forgive Jennifer for betraying my trust."

Forgiveness is something you do for yourself because holding a grudge makes it hard to enjoy life. When you forgive someone who has hurt you, it doesn't mean you have to be friends, like them, or even tell them you have forgiven them. Forgiveness means letting go of a hurtful situation and moving on with your own happiness. Do you know someone you need to forgive today?

Mind Your Manners

A guy once said to me, "You say 'please' and 'thank you' too much."

"No I don't," I argued. "It's polite. Haven't you ever heard of manners?"

"Manners don't mean anything, and politeness is just fake," he replied.

Many people underestimate the power of politeness. Manners go far beyond simply saying "please" and "thank you" or keeping your elbows off the table when you eat. When you mind your manners, you show other people that you respect them and aren't just thinking of yourself. For example, thanking your friend's parents for having you over for dinner lets them know that you appreciate what they have done for you. They will admire your politeness because a little bit of manners goes a long way with parents.

Today, use your best manners. Remember that politeness can be a key to success, especially when dealing with adults.

Get Rid of an Abusive Boyfriend

Having a boyfriend is so important for some girls that we sometimes stay in unhealthy relationships because we like the security of having a boyfriend. However, having a boyfriend is not worth risking your personal safety or your mental well-being. If your boyfriend is aggressive toward you or others, or if he kicks things and punches holes in walls, he is not a good guy to be with. Your boyfriend is potentially dangerous if he wants all of your attention or tries to take you away from your family and friends, if he makes you check in with him, or if he bosses you around by telling you whom you should and shouldn't talk to. You should be concerned if he's extremely jealous when you talk to other guys, blames you for the bad things he does and says, calls you names and makes fun of you, excessively drinks or uses drugs, or has an explosive temper.

If you have a tiny feeling that something isn't quite right with your boyfriend, get out of the relationship immediately. The longer you stay with an abusive, overprotective boyfriend, the more self-destructive you are being.

Hormones Galore

Do you ever feel like an emotional basket case—one day you are perfectly happy, and the next day the most trivial things can throw you into a fit of tears? Have you ever had your face break out despite the fact you take excellent care of your skin? These things happen because of hormones.

You may hear adults talk about how teenagers' hormones are raging. It's true—right now ours are out of control. Our bodies are growing and changing at such a rapid pace that our hormones are working overtime. This is why you may find yourself feeling depressed, irritated, or without energy. Hormones may also cause your skin to break out or your hair to be extra oily.

Next time you find yourself in one of these frustrating situations, remember, it's probably your hormones.

It's Not a Disaster

It was senior year, and Homecoming was going to be great. I was going with Derek, my best guy friend since seventh grade, and a group of my closest friends.

The phone rang the night before the dance. "I can't go to Homecoming," Derek blurted.

"What?" I asked.

"I got caught with alcohol at the football game," he said, "and I got suspended. I can't go to the dance."

I wanted to scream at him. How could he ruin my last homecoming ever? Tears filled my eyes as I hung up. What was I going to do? I thought about it and realized that I could either throw a fit and make Derek feel worse than he already did, or find another solution.

So I called all my friends, they found a guy who didn't have a date, and he and I went together at the last minute.

Life never goes according to plan. There will always be switching, changing, and rearranging to do. Don't let small hold-ups turn into major disasters. When things don't go your way, there is always a solution besides moping or making a scene, but it's up to you to find it.

Lay Off the Guilt Trips

Have you ever put a guilt trip on your parents? I have, saying something like, "Kendra's mom always buys her new clothes," or, "Everyone else's parents are letting them go to the concert," or, "I'm the only person at school who doesn't have a pager."

If you feel like your parents don't provide you with everything you want, you need to learn the difference between which things are really important to you and which things are just fads that will soon pass. You may want to consider getting a job and finance your wants on your own. If work isn't an option, you may want to cut down on your "needs."

Today, give your parents a break—they are doing the best they can. Maybe they don't have enough money to afford all the things your friends' families do, but when you put guilt trips on them, it makes them feel terrible that they can't provide you with all you desire.

Lose the Labels

My friend Jayme and I always had completely different groups of friends. I was a "preppy" and she was a "hippie." When we went out together, we always joked that people must wonder what we were doing together because we had totally different styles. Even though we hung out with different people, I considered her one of my closest friends through junior high and high school. I needed her friendship in a way that my best friends couldn't fill.

Teens label everyone. Jocks, stoners, dorks, or snobs—everyone belongs to some "group." You may be able to tell a lot about a person by his or her friends, but clumping people into superficial categories will leave you making a lot of incorrect assumptions about them. Cheerleaders aren't necessarily airheads, and girls who get good grades don't always study all the time. You may be surprised at the wonderful friendships you'll make if you get to know someone individually instead of making judgments about them based on the "group" they belong to.

Falling for a Nerd

Have you ever had a crush on a guy but didn't tell anyone because he was called a "nerd"? Often we get so caught up in what a guy looks like or his social status that we decide he's "undateable" before we even get to know him. Everyone has different tastes in guys, and the qualities that draw you to a guy will not be the same qualities your friends find attractive.

Every girl gets a crush on an "uncool" guy at least once, but she's often scared to admit it because she's afraid she'll be made fun of. Don't feel embarrassed to pursue the guy you like. He may be an awesome guy, and then you can help other girls see that it's cool to fall for a nerd!

Always Make Time for Introductions

Here's a good rule to remember: Always introduce your friends to your parents. "My parents are so embarrassing!" you argue. "They'll say something stupid, ask weird questions, act foolish, and make me totally uncomfortable!" Sometimes introducing your friends to your parents isn't the easiest thing to do because parents can be embarrassing, but risking a little embarrassment will be well worth it.

Now that you are older, your parents are no longer as involved in your friendships as they had been when you were younger. You are meeting many new people, and this may make your parents a little nervous. They will wonder, "Who is my daughter hanging out with? What are her new friends like?" If you take time to introduce your parents to your new friends, you make them feel included in your life and put their worries at ease. The more you let your parents get to know your friends, the more freedom they will give you. Your parents will feel more comfortable letting you go out if they know the people you'll be with.

Proud to Flirt

"You're such a flirt, Amanda!" my friends always told me.

"I am not!" I would argue. I'm just friendly."

"No, you're not *just* friendly, you're a flirt," they'd say, "and you flirt with every guy!"

It's true, I'm a flirt. I guess it's just part of my nature, and I particularly enjoyed it during my teens. Even when I had a boyfriend, I still flirted with other guys. I'm not a tease or trying to get attention from guys, I just like to flirt.

Flirting is fun because it's harmless. You aren't really putting yourself out on the line because flirting with a guy doesn't automatically mean that you want to date him. Flirting adds a little excitement to your day, so today, be proud to be flirtatious!

Boo! It's Halloween!

Today is Halloween, the day of costumes, spooks, and, of course, chocolate. As a child, I looked forward to dressing up and parading around the neighborhood with the other ghosts, goblins, witches, and princesses, collecting candy at each house. No matter how old I get, Halloween continues to be a day of mystery for me. There is a certain eeriness in the air on this day, not an evil eeriness, just a sense of excitement.

It's fun to be a little scared at the eeriness of Halloween. Wear a mask and put up decorations, or watch a scary movie and get yourself spooked. Get into the Halloween spirit, whether you are out trick-or-treating with friends, heading to a Halloween party, or staying home to pass out candy.

In November. . .

Discover classical music. Try Mozart, Vivaldi, Beethoven, or Bach. You will find the relaxing melodies provide a nice change of pace from your usual radio station.

Watch the Macy's Thanksgiving Day parade.

Play with your hair. Cut it, color it, or just style it a new way.

Careless Wishes

In high school, I drove an '86 white Subaru hatchback that my friends called "The Egg." It was a good car—low mileage, clean interior, and no dents or scratches—but it wasn't good enough for me. I secretly cursed my car, hoping it would get stolen or hit in a parking lot so I could get a new one. I wanted something red and sporty that zipped around corners and had a nice stereo.

My wish came true during my senior year of high school when I hit another car and totaled my little white Egg. Instead of feeling overjoyed by the chance to get a new car, I was heartbroken. I felt spoiled and careless. I no longer wanted a new car, I wanted my little Egg.

Why don't we appreciate what we have until it's gone? Today, be grateful for what you have instead of focusing on the things you lack. Don't wish for things to be different or for a new wardrobe, a hot boyfriend, a loud stereo, or no siblings. Be very careful what you wish for because, to your dismay, it just might come true.

I Don't Like Her

If you were to make a list of everyone you don't like, how long would your list be? Five, twelve, or maybe twenty people? There will always be people whom you don't like, who get on your nerves, who irritate you, who disgust you, or whom you don't respect.

In the same way that you don't like everyone, there are some people who won't like you. It hurts when we find out someone dislikes us. However, just because one person dislikes you doesn't mean everyone dislikes you. You will always find people who don't like you; maybe they are jealous of you, feel threatened by you, or had a bad first impression. Trying to make everyone like you is an impossible task and a huge waste of time. When you get the feeling you're on somebody's "hate list," don't worry about it, stress over it, or try to change his or her mind. Move on. Focus your energy on the people who like you for you, because they have the opinions that count!

Explore Religion

I learned a lot as a teen by observing my friends experiment with different religious beliefs. I had Mormon friends, one who became a Buddhist nun after graduation, and another who didn't believe in any God. Some of my friends were Christians since birth, while others became Christian during high school. My trip to Indonesia showed me how the Hindu religion was tightly woven into the daily lives of the Balinese people.

Maybe you've grown up going to the same church your whole life, maybe you know nothing about religion, or maybe you're somewhere in the middle. Whatever your religious upbringing, it is important to think deeply about it. Is there a God? Why do you believe what you do? Talk to people of different religions to learn about their beliefs, or attend different church services. You don't have to become a member of a different religion to learn something from that religion.

Learning about different religions opens your mind to new ways of thinking. You may find that no other religion is right, or you may discover something new. Exploring different religious beliefs will give you a greater understanding of people and the world.

Why Doesn't He Like to Talk on the Phone?

Sitting impatiently at my desk, I chewed anxiously on the cap of my pen as butterflies swarmed in my stomach. Checking the clock for the third time, I was annoyed only a minute had passed. I put the phone to my ear to make sure it was still working, then grabbed a magazine from my bookshelf. Just as I began to flip through the pages, the phone rang; instantly, I was standing at my desk. I rested my hand on the receiver, but didn't answer the phone until the third ring. "Hello," I said, sounding as casual as possible. Disappointment filled me when I heard the voice on the other end. "Oh, hi, Mom. It's you."

Why is it that we wait for the phone to ring, and when it finally does, it is never him?

Guys don't like to talk on the phone, a lesson that took me many years to learn. It all goes back to the hunter-gatherer days. Girls are gatherers; we like to talk on the phone for hours, collecting information through our conversations. Boys are hunters who go straight in for the kill. They only call when they have a specific purpose.

Grandparents Know All the Dirt

What do you think of your grandparents? Do they spoil you with presents every time they see you or brag to their friends about all your amazing accomplishments? I bet you don't know that your grandparents are a wonderful source of good gossip. Your grandparents have all the dirt on your parents. They can tell you about your dad getting suspended from school in the tenth grade or the funny story behind why your mother refuses to ride in elevators.

Ask your grandparents what your parents were like as teens. Your parents will begin to take on a new form in your eyes when you hear about all the crazy things they did when they were your age.

With a Little Help from a Friend

When a friend says to you, "I'm in trouble. I need your help," you may get a little worried. Helping a friend through a hard time can bring the two of you closer, but it can also be scary because you may not be ready or able to take on his or her problem by yourself.

The most important thing to remember when helping a friend is that you should do only what you feel comfortable doing. Listen to your friend's problem, and tell him or her what you would do in the same situation. If you think it's a problem that the two of you can handle without outside help, go for it, but getting yourself in trouble to help a friend isn't worth it.

Whatever the problem may be—boys, school, family, drugs, or stealing—when a friend comes to you seeking help, it's a sign that he or she trusts you. Do what you can to help, and be sensitive to your friend's feelings, but if it feels too big for the both of you, go to a trusted adult.

A Friend in Need

One of my high school friends had a drinking problem. He got drunk every weekend and would even drink at home by himself sometimes. We all knew he had a problem, but felt uncomfortable saying anything to him, so we watched as he slowly went downhill.

It is always okay to tell your friends that you are worried about them. Sometimes a friend won't ask for help even if he or she needs and wants it. Maybe her drinking is a way she can escape her sadness, or his constant troublemaking at school is a cry for attention. Letting your friend know that you care could be all he or she needs to hear to stop a small problem from turning into a disaster. Say, "I am worried about you. You don't seem to be acting like yourself lately. Is there anything I can do?" Your friend may not open up to you right away, and he or she may even get defensive or upset with you for asking. If you are patient and loving, your friend will soon come around.

Sometimes You Have to Turn Your Back on a Friend

You've done all you can to help your friend with her problem. You've listened, offered advice, been patient, and helped in every way you know how, but your friend only seems to be getting deeper into trouble. If your friend refuses to deal with his or her problems in a positive way, it is time for you to move on.

If you feel comfortable, talk to a school counselor and let him or her know about your friend's problem, or if you think it's necessary, tell her parents. Distance yourself from your friend until he or she overcomes the problem. You don't have to completely end your friendship, but it's important that you don't let your friend's big problems drag you down. Watch out for your own well-being if you feel you've put all the energy you can into helping your friend. Sometimes the best way to help people is to distance yourself, find new friends, and show them that ignoring their problems is an unhealthy way to live.

You can only help someone to a certain point before it begins to wear on you. In the end, your friend must be willing to help him- or herself.

Grieve for the People You Love

Death can be a hard concept for a teenager to grasp. Life stretches ahead of you, open and full of possibility. Somewhere along the line, you realize that death is a part of life. Death has probably touched you in some way, maybe through the death of a family member, friend, neighbor, pet, or even your own parent. With the onset of winter and the upcoming holidays, you may find yourself missing people who have died.

Today, grieve for the people you have lost. Cry for your mother or your best friend who died. It is okay to stay in bed all day, to be slow, and feel pain, even if the person died years ago; let yourself miss his or her presence in your life. Remember that the road to healing winds through pain, anguish, sickness, and many tears.

That Happened to Me Once, Too!

"I've had a terrible day," I told my friend. "I failed the calculus test, and my mom and I got in a fight."

"At least you aren't sick!" she replied. "I've got a bad cold but I can't miss school because of my two tests. My mom and I got in a fight last night, too. She can be so irritating that I swear she's out to make my life miserable."

Have you ever gone to a friend because you need someone to listen to you, but then she ends up talking about her problems?

We all fall into Ego-Listening sometimes. When someone comes to us with a problem, we compare that experience to our own by saying, "I know how you feel," or, "That happened to me once." Turning the conversation to your problems makes the other person feel like his or her situation is inferior to yours.

Today, when you listen, avoid making ego-centered comments, giving advice, or judging. Ask questions and show you're interested in hearing about others' lives. Your friends will appreciate you more if you're a good listener.

Gatsby's Great Smile

In F. Scott Fitzgerald's famous novel *The Great Gatsby*, the main character, Nick, embarrassed himself at Jay Gatsby's party. Instead of laughing at Nick and making him feel even more humiliated, Gatsby "smiled understandingly. It was one of those rare smiles with a quality of reassurance in it. . . . he believed in you as you would like to believe in yourself and assured you that it had precisely the impression of you that, at your best, you hoped to convey."

We all know what it feels like to be totally embarrassed about something—when someone announces to your whole lunch table that you have a crush on this older guy; when you fall flat on your face in the middle of a crowded hall; or when your teacher asks you a question in class and you give an answer that is completely wrong. Think about how much worse you feel when someone makes fun of you for whatever embarrassing moment you've just experienced.

Today, when you notice that somebody is embarrassed or uncomfortable about something, don't tease. Instead, give them Gatsby's great smile or a supportive comment.

Ditched

On the night of the '50s dance at school, I suggested to my girlfriends that we go together dressed like the Pink Ladies from the movie *Grease*. After a few girls went to buy pink tee shirts, I discovered that they had planned to go without me—they didn't even get me a shirt.

I bawled my eyes out. How could they leave me out? I was hurt but determined not to let them ruin my night. My mom helped me get decked out in '50s attire, and I drove myself to the dance. Despite feeling betrayed, I danced, socialized, and went out for ice cream with different friends after the dance.

People will betray you, even during your teenage years. Friends will stab you in the back, leave you out, or hurt your feelings. You can't let other people ruin your life or your good time. If friends leave you out of their plans, keep smiling, and go anyway. Make new friends, and when you are hurting, force yourself to have a good time. Eventually, you will feel better, you will learn who your true friends are, and you will have fun without having to try.

Feeling Lonely

Sometimes we feel painfully alone. We all try to escape from it by surrounding ourselves with people, getting involved with clubs, talking on the phone, or watching TV. No matter how fast we run away, our loneliness always catches up with us. Loneliness can make its way through all of our friends, family, and acquaintances and gets into our hearts. Even when you are surrounded by people, you can still feel like nobody cares about you or really understands you.

Loneliness isn't something that goes away easily. As Dr. Seuss says, "Whether you like it or not, alone will be something you'll be quite a lot." You'll have the same lonely times at age thirty that you do now. People will come and go during your lifetime, but you are the only person who will be there for you all the time.

The only way to ward off loneliness is to invite it in. Accept your lonely feelings as normal and healthy. Ask yourself for help. Lean on yourself, talk to yourself as a friend, and then lift yourself up. When you face your fear of being alone, you won't be so upset when it creeps up on you again.

Humor Your Mother

The first thing my mother wants to do whenever I walk through the door is hang out and talk, whether it's after school or at midnight. When all I want to do is to go to my room and listen to music, my mother has a list of fifty questions prepared: "How was your day? Did you have fun? Who did you talk to? Are you hungry?" Even when she's finished with questions, she has news to tell me. "Did you see how the neighbors are remodeling their house? It's going to be huge!" Her list of things for me to do always comes next. "Put your laundry away; the laundry room is a pigsty! I need you to help me carry these boxes out to the garage tomorrow morning. Could you hand me my glasses? I want to read you this newspaper article I think you will find interesting."

If you are irritated by your mother's frequent questions, remember, she asks them because she misses being part of your life. Tell her a little bit. You don't have to divulge all your information; just give her an overview so she feels like she's included in your exciting life.

Cry Me a River

Have you ever noticed how good you feel after crying? Crying releases tension and pent-up feelings and then floods our bodies with feel-good hormones.

There are many reasons to cry, and just about anything can strike that place in your heart and set your tears into action. You can cry when you are sad about something or when you are happy. You can cry when something touches your heart or somebody does something nice for you, and you can cry when you hurt yourself or get sick or stressed out. Sometimes a certain song or painting makes me cry. You can even cry for no particular reason at all.

If the urge to cry strikes you, let it out. There is something cleansing about letting your tears out, and you always feel refreshed after a good, long cry.

When You Hate Someone, Pray for Them

I pounded my fist on the table. "I hate Michelle!! She's so mean. I hate, hate, hate her! I wish she would die." My face got red even as I thought about her, the girl who ruined so much of my eighth grade year. She stole guys I liked, made up rumors about me, and glared at me when I walked down the hall. Only bad thoughts and mean wishes consumed me when I thought about her.

A year later, I began to find out more about Michelle. She had two alcoholic parents, her father was abusive, and her brother did more drugs than I had ever heard of. Michelle had so many negative things happening to her that the last thing she needed was me wishing more bad for her.

Today, say a prayer for someone you hate. People are mean because other people have been mean to them. Positive things will happen when you pray for others, especially those you don't like.

Write a List of Thanks

Since Thanksgiving is coming soon, it's time to focus on all you are grateful for. Throughout the year, we get so caught up thinking about everything we don't have that we forget to remember we already have so much.

What has happened in this past year that you are thankful for? What experiences have you had? Who has helped you? What has your family done for you? How have you helped yourself? Write down everything, big and small. Decorate your list if you like, but add to it over the next few weeks and hang it somewhere you can read it daily, and remind yourself of all that has gone right in your life. You can even suggest that your whole family make a gratitude list so you can each share something from it on Thanksgiving. When you write a list of thanks, you'll realize you have more to be grateful for than you ever realized.

Send Letters of Thanks

Thanksgiving is about acknowledging all we are grateful for in our lives. The best way to do this is to thank the people who have contributed to making your life wonderful. This time of year is perfect for recognizing the people we take for granted as well as people who have made a big impact on our lives.

Today, send letters of thanks. Write to anyone you want to say thank you to—your best friends, teachers, parents, siblings, extended family, boyfriend, piano teacher, tennis coach, the lady at the deli who always makes your sandwich for you, the guy who helped you study for your German final, or your neighbor who helped you find your dog when she got lost. Whether you write a simple thank you note or a long letter of gratitude, giving thanks to others is what gives life to the spirit of Thanksgiving.

Homeward Bound

You need a vacation in a major way, but it doesn't look like your parents are making plans for a family trip in tropical paradise anytime soon. That's okay, because you can have a vacation right in your own home.

Pick a weekend night and have your own personal vacation. Make an itinerary of fun things you want to do, like watching your favorite movie, taking a long bubble bath, reading a book, or dancing around your room. Remind yourself that you are on vacation for a night—no worrying about homework, thinking about friendship problems, or fighting with your family is allowed. All you are allowed to do is stay home, relax, and do whatever you enjoy.

Caught Without a Date

You are still without a date for the upcoming dance, and time is running out. You're feeling terrible, completely unattractive, and you're sure you're the only girl who hasn't been asked to the dance yet.

When you find yourself in this situation, you need to realize that you have several options. Believe it or not, guys are complete cowards when it comes to girls, so maybe you should do the asking for yourself. Just think of all the *guys* who are left without dates because they are too nervous to ask. You can also round up all the girls who are in the same position and go together in a group. Dances that become girls' night out can be the most fun because there aren't any pressures of being with a date. You can also simply forget the dance altogether and stay home.

Make up your mind to be happy no matter what decision you make. Don't get down on yourself because there will be many more dances to come. Just because your dream guy didn't ask you to this one doesn't mean that you won't have a hot date for the next one.

Not Everyone Can Take a Joke

Have you ever made a teasing comment that hurt someone's feelings? While you may be the type of person who likes to be sarcastic and joke around, not everyone can take a joke or handle being teased. It's important to be careful about how you joke. You may say something in fun, but the other person may take it personally, especially if you hit their most sensitive subject.

You don't have to be serious all the time, but you can learn to be sensitive to other people's vulnerable spots. Pay attention to how others respond to your joking, and if they seem uncomfortable, it's best to stop. Not everyone can relate to your sense of humor, and not everyone can tell when you're being serious or silly.

Griping and Moaning

My class and I took a month-long trip to Hawaii. It was beautiful! Every day, we saw warm sun, blue ocean, soft sand, and bright flowers. We were in paradise, but for some reason, people were still complaining. They griped about the food we ate, the cabins we stayed in, and the other people in the group. People were so busy complaining that I wondered if they ever took time to recognize the beauty that surrounded us in every direction.

Many girls complain simply for the sake of complaining or as a way to feel connected to one another. Pay attention to yourself today: Can you make it through the entire day without grumbling? I bet it's much harder than you think. If you make a vow to stop mindless complaining and refuse to let others' negativity bring you down, you will begin to notice all the wonderful things around you.

All You Have to Do Is Dream

What problems are you confronting in your life right now? What are your worried about? Is there an issue you aren't exactly sure how to handle? Try using your dreams to help you solve your problems.

Tonight, before you go to bed, think about a problem you're trying to solve or something you're worried about. Write down what you're hoping to figure out, like "How should I fix the fight I'm in with Emma?" or, "Why am I feeling so sad lately? What would make me feel better?" Set the piece of paper next to your bed, and as you fall asleep, think about your question. A solution will often come to you while you sleep, because then your mind has the ability to think without being censored by you, and your subconscious mind is free to expose itself. If you do get help from your dream, be sure to thank your unconscious mind so it will help you again.

The Phone Is for More Than Just Talking

In 1876, a person at the company Western Union said that the telephone "has too many shortcomings to be seriously considered as a means of communication. The device is totally of no value to us." Western Union obviously didn't consult a teenage girl when making this statement.

The phone is an amazing device. It keeps you up to date on anything that may happen while you are away from school, allows you to easily make plans for Friday night, and lets you quickly consult your friends on any topic you may need advising on. The phone is not just a communication device, it's a tool that can enhance your social life and is also a means of entertainment that keeps you engaged for hours.

The next time your parents get mad at you for talking on the phone, tell them you're not just talking, you're staying connected to the world and giving your social skills a much-needed fine tuning.

Have a **Seinfeld** Day

My favorite show of all time is *Seinfeld*. I have every episode on tape and watch them over and over again. I never get sick of the wacky things that Elaine, George, Kramer, and Jerry do. The most wonderful thing about *Seinfeld* is that it finds comedy in the events that happen to us every day. It's a show about nothing, yet it's so hysterical.

Today, see your life as a sitcom. There is comedy all around you—just open your eyes and see it! What can you find that's funny about yourself, your family, friends, and strangers you see on the street? I guarantee you that when you watch your ordinary routine, you will find comedy in it that will leave you shouting, "This could be a *Seinfeld* episode!"

Healthy Escapes

Wanting to escape from the hard times you're having is normal when you are sad and lonely. Many teens turn to drugs and alcohol, yet there are better ways to escape from your pain, ways that will let you forget your hurt *and* help you heal.

Today, make a list of healthy escapes you can use the next time you're feeling sad. Fill it with things that help you feel better. I turn on my favorite music and paint a picture, losing my worries in the bright colors, or I strap on my rollerblades and skate for hours in the park, mending my heart a little with every glide. Other times, I soak in a bath, retreat into a book, or crawl into bed and cry myself to sleep.

Downing a beer or getting high with your friends may make your pain go away, but the effect is only temporary. When your numbness wears off, your hurt will still be there. Next time you are feeling down in the dumps, be strong and turn to a healthy escape, and you will be one step closer to happiness.

Hold On to Your Girlfriends

My guy friends in high school had a motto they stuck to religiously: "Bros before hoes." Although the wording is far from tasteful, the meaning carries a great deal of importance—friends are important and should never be ditched for girlfriends.

Why don't girls have a motto like this? It seems quite the opposite for girls—we will drop everything, even our best friends, for a guy. This tendency isn't smart. Our girlfriends are the ones who listened to us talk about how much we liked him and reassured us that he liked us too, and they will probably be the ones who listen to us cry when we get into a fight with him.

Although your thoughts may be turned to your boyfriend most of the time, it is important that you continue to devote time to hanging out with your girlfriends. Keep eating lunch with your girlfriends, talking on the phone, and spending at least one weekend night with them. If you only go to them when you need help or when your guy isn't available, they will feel used and will stop thinking of you as a friend.

What Do Your Parents Think about That?

When I was thirteen, I never wanted to have anything to do with my mom. I didn't like telling her about my life and never asked for her advice about my problems. As I got older, I began to realize that my mom was right about a lot of things. Since she is my mother, she knows me well and understands why I act the way I do. Now, whenever I ask my mom's opinion, she gives me the best advice and always seems to know exactly what I should do.

It may not always seem like it, but your parents are on your side. They were teenagers once, too, and although times have changed, teenage experiences have stayed very much the same. Try asking your parents for their advice and see what they have to say. You don't necessarily have to do what they say, but you may be pleasantly surprised to find that your parents might offer you the perfect solution to your problems.

Be Confident in Your Looks

If you think guys won't like you because you aren't the prettiest girl in school, think again. Guys don't only go for the prettiest girls. I have heard many guys say that the way a girl carries herself is more important than her looks. My eighteen-year-old friend Nate once said, "I like it when a girl is confident about her looks. It's a big turn-off when girls say things like, 'I'm so ugly,' or, 'Look at how bad my hair looks today!' Even a super hot girl can make herself ugly by complaining about the way she looks."

So what if you aren't the most beautiful girl around? Love the way you look. Be confident that you are pretty, and the boys will notice. As my friend Justin says, "Every single girl has something beautiful about her. I wish more girls would flaunt what they know is pretty instead of focusing on their imperfections."

Be Approachable

My mother's friend had a daughter named Crystal. Although we went to the same school, we never talked at school. We got along great when our mothers brought us together, but when we passed each other at school, I acted like I didn't know her. One day when Crystal was at my house with her mother, she said to me, "Don't worry, I'll never talk to you at school. You're more popular than I am, and I know you wouldn't want people to see you talking to me." I felt terrible when I heard this. Was I so snobby and wrapped up in popularity that I had made Crystal, a girl who knew me well, feel like she couldn't approach me to say hello?

Today, ditch your school's class system and talk to everyone. Be approachable instead of intimidating, and remember that the true definition of popular is being friends with everyone, even people who are less popular than you.

In December. . .

Put holiday lights up in your room.

Have a seasonal film festival. Invite your friends over to watch movies like Miracle on 34th Street, It's a Wonderful Life, *and any other holiday movies you love. Drink hot chocolate or eggnog, and eat holiday cookies.*

Write thank-you's to people who have given you gifts and have helped make your holidays special.

Bring in the New Year with your close friends. Create a New Year's tradition, like drinking cider or going to a special place to share your New Year's resolutions with each other.

Remember That
Mom's Human, Too

Sometimes I just couldn't get along with my mother. No matter how hard I tried, I couldn't seem to keep myself from fighting with her. I would yell at her when she said something that irritated me, or snap when she asked a question I didn't feel like answering. I always felt terrible for being mean to her, but the next time she did something that got on my nerves, I would do it again.

Getting along with Mom is much easier said than done. I always loved my mom, but there were many times during my teens when I hated her at the same time, without really knowing why.

If this is happening to you, try to remember that your mother has feelings and that she gets hurt, angry, and sad, just like you. The next time she does something that irritates you, take a deep breath before responding. Thinking before you act will help you avoid outbursts of anger that you will regret later. Be patient with yourself and your mother. The two of you are learning how relate to each other during this new time in your life.

I Hate My Life

Your hair is not cooperating, but it's not just a matter of having a bad hair day. You missed the bus to school this morning, you forgot to do your homework last night, your best friend is ignoring you, there's nothing good to eat for lunch, and you are just feeling terrible. Today is not just a bad hair day, it's a bad life day.

We all have days like this, and during the dark winter months, you may find that there are more bad life days than usual. It's good to have a day of self-pity once in a while, as long as you don't let it take over. The winter can be depressing and take its toll on your spirit. When you find yourself feeling down, irritated, and ready to scream, declare that day an "I hate my life" day.

I'm Sorry

One time I told my friend Katie I thought our friend Erica was being a snob. Katie immediately went to Erica, telling her what I had said, and then Erica got mad and refused to talk to me. Although I had a reason for my comment, and there would have never been a problem if Katie had kept her mouth closed, I had still hurt Erica's feelings.

Many times when we do something like this and hurt someone, we try to cover it up by saying, "That's not how I meant it." We may even get defensive and say, "Well, you were being a brat!" When you've done something that has hurt another person, the best thing to do is apologize. You don't need to explain yourself or try to sugar-coat what you said. Just admit to the mistake and let the other person know that you didn't mean to be hurtful. Sometimes the best thing to say when you have hurt another person is simply, "I'm sorry."

Why Won't You Forgive Me?

Have you ever apologized to someone for something that you have done wrong, but the other person refuses to forgive you? Sometimes it may take a while for a friend to forgive you because when you hurt their feelings, you betray their trust. Show your friend you understand you've messed up and that you can still be trusted. Refrain from comments like, "I said I'm sorry. I don't understand why you are still mad at me," or, "Sara is totally overreacting about what I said." Instead, give your friend a card that says you miss her friendship, or invite her to talk with you about what is still upsetting her.

It can take a while for your friend to trust you again and for your friendship to be rebuilt. You cannot make someone forgive you, and they may choose not to. Once you have done your best to mend your mistake, let go.

What? You Don't Believe in Santa Claus?

Okay, so you have long since learned that there is no jolly old man who rides in a sleigh pulled by reindeer and scoots down your chimney on Christmas leaving a bundle of gifts under your tree. That doesn't mean there isn't a Santa Claus. As Francis P. Church wrote, "Alas! How dreary would be the world if there was no Santa Claus! . . . There would be no childlike faith then, no poetry, no romance to make tolerable this existence."

Santa is everywhere—he is the personification of the spirit of Christmas. During Christmastime, our hearts fill with the desire to give love, and we sit around with friends and family joyfully singing songs like "Santa Claus Is Coming to Town." Even when we go to sleep on Christmas Eve, our dreams are filled with a little bit more magic than any other time of year. As long as these things exist, so does Santa.

You are never too old to bask in the Christmas spirit, and you are never too old to believe in Santa Claus!

Take Responsibility for Your Feelings

Many of us find it incredibly hard to be aware of our feelings and actions. It is difficult for us to acknowledge our weaknesses and insecurities, so we simply choose to ignore them and act without thinking. If you are jealous of a friend, you may say to others, "Cassey isn't that great. She acts a lot different when I'm alone with her. Besides, I don't think that she's that pretty." You may get really mad at a friend and yell, "You are totally overreacting!" when you're the one freaking out.

These are times you project your feelings onto other people to help ease your negative feelings about yourself. If you convince people your friend isn't as wonderful as everyone thinks, then you look like the better person. If it is someone else who is overreacting, then you look like the sensible one. Most people do these things without even knowing why.

Today, if you find yourself saying something bad about another person, stop and ask yourself, "Is what I'm saying true, or am I saying it because I'm jealous?" Admit your negative feelings and realize that you are acting on them in a hurtful way.

Create the Perfect Gift

Have you found yourself caught in the holiday scramble to get gifts for your family and friends? When you are on a low budget, finding the perfect gift can be stressful and take the joy out of giving. A gift doesn't have to be expensive to be meaningful, and handmade gifts are usually the most special because they show that you put time and effort into the gift, instead of just running to the mall and looking for something to buy.

What are some homemade gifts you could give? Make a tape of music you know she'll love for a friend; create a photo collage and frame it; make cookies using a flower-shaped cookie cutter, and put them in a flower pot that you painted; paint a friendship quote on a wooden picture frame; or give a book of homemade coupons for "One free car wash" or "A home-cooked dinner of your choice." The ideas for homemade gifts are countless. Put your creative energies to work, and you are guaranteed to create the ideal gift.

You've Got the Magic

In the fairy tale "The Frog Prince," a lovely princess is courted by a frog who insists that she kiss him. When she finally does, he magically turns into a prince and the two live happily ever after. In the turnaround story, "Princess Smarty Pants," the princess kisses a handsome prince, turns him into a frog, and lives happily ever after without him!

I like the newer version of this story. Another person cannot give you whatever you are missing in life by making magical things happen. It is up to you to use your inner powers to make your wishes come true. Find your inner strength; don't count on friends to lift your spirits or on guys to make you feel attractive. Remember, whether it is a prince or a frog you choose to love, the magic lies in you.

Life Is a Balancing Act

A teacher once told me that life is like walking on the rim of a bowl with one thing pulling from the inside and its opposite pulling at you from the outside. The key is not to let one thing pull at you so much that you fall off the rim in either direction; instead, you should remain steady and balanced between the two things.

We live in a world of contradictions. We are continually pulled between work and play, friends and family, and sadness and joy; it is your job to figure out how to create harmony among so many opposites. If you get off balance, your life becomes filled with turmoil. If you ate only vegetables all the time, you would never know the delicious taste of desserts, but if you ate only desserts, you would make yourself sick.

If you are feeling a little out of sync because you've been giving a lot of attention to one area of your life, balance yourself out by devoting time to the area you have neglected.

Daddy's Little Girl

Growing up, I always dreamed of being Daddy's little girl. I longed for my dad to coach my soccer team, teach me to drive, and put my boyfriends through the third degree before they took me out. Daddy's little girl was never a role I got to play. I scored game-winning goals, learned how to drive, and watched birthdays come and go without my father there to cheer me on. My dad chose not to take part in my life.

There will be many people whose presence you long for in your life, but not everyone will be there for you. Parents leave, friends betray you, family members die; it's all part of life. Accepting the loss of someone you care about is hard, especially during the holidays, when we are supposed to be surrounded by people we care about.

Holidays are also about cherishing the abundance in your life. Today, focus on the people who do care about you. Notice the love you have and give love back. Once you begin to focus on the wonderful people in your life, the hole left by that missing person will grow smaller.

Everyone Has
Something to Give

One summer, my friend traveled with a group of teens to a small village in Mexico so they could build a house for a poor family who was living in a shack made of cardboard and scraps of wood. When the house was completed, the family was so grateful that my friend decided to do it again the next year. When her group returned the following summer, they found the first family living in the old cardboard shack again. The family had turned their house into a church for the entire village to use!

Even if you think you have nothing, you always have *something* to give. Giving isn't about money; it's about sharing with others before thinking of yourself. This holiday season, be generous—give your time to volunteer work, some food to the homeless, or a smile to someone who's sad.

Shhhh! It's a Quiet Day

We often feel stressed out and complain that we really don't know ourselves because we rarely take the time to be quiet and listen to what's going on inside of us. Today, have a celebration of silence. Go outside and listen to the sounds of nature, or sit in your room and see what thoughts come to mind. Turn off the radio, the television, your pager, the computer, and the ringer on your phone and just be quiet.

Even when the world around you is loud and hectic, you can have quiet inside yourself. Many people are scared of silence and get nervous instead of quiet, but it is important to get past that fear. Instead of running to the phone or television when you don't have anything else to do, go for a walk alone or write in your journal. You'll be amazed at what can happen when you take time to be quiet and listen to yourself. After you've spent some quiet time, you'll be able to study better for a test or think of a solution to a problem that's been bothering you.

Got to Earn That Trust

Are you feeling like your parents don't trust you? Does your mother insist on knowing where you are and whom you are with at every moment? Has your father laid down the strictest rules possible in your house while your friends can do whatever they want?

Before you fly off the deep end of rebellion, think for a moment. Have you given your parents a reason not to trust you? Trust is something that must be earned. Many girls try to get more freedom by breaking rules, not calling when they say they will, and lying to their parents. The best way to earn freedom is by following the rules that your parents have placed in front of you. Once you become trustworthy, you can explain to your parents why you think the rules need to be relaxed a bit.

Today, act trustworthy. You will see that when you have earned your parents' trust, you will be given much more freedom to do as you please.

They Still Don't Trust Me

You've done all you can to show your parents you can be trusted. You follow rules, never lie, and are squeaky clean, but your parents are still suspicious.

Your first reaction may be to rebel. "My parents don't trust me whether I am good or not, so I may as well be bad," you may think. Although rebellion may get you what you want right now, it won't make you happy in the long run and will make your parents even more strict.

Today, look at the situation through your parents' eyes. Why are they acting the way they are? Maybe your mother made a big mistake as a teen and is trying to save you from doing the same. Maybe your father isn't quite sure how much freedom to give to a daughter, so he becomes overprotective. Talk to your parents to figure out why they have given you so little room to move. Explain to them that you've done everything you can to show you're trustworthy, and you don't understand why they continue to be so strict.

A Diversity of Celebration

America is a country of diversity, and the holiday season provides a perfect example of this diversity. When people immigrate to America, they bring their culture, their holidays, and their celebrations. Christmas is the most common holiday, but not the only holiday, that is celebrated in America during the month of December.

Today, learn about the many different holidays that are celebrated around our country. Hanukkah is the celebration of the survival of the Jewish religion. Kwanzaa is the African American celebration of family and black culture, and Mexicans commemorate the journey of Mary and Joseph from Nazareth to Bethlehem with Posadas.

Find out how different people celebrate the holidays. Even with our diverse culture, there is a spirit that comes alive during December and unites all people, no matter what their beliefs.

Holiday Light Celebration

The thing I love the most about the holidays is the lights. Seeing neighborhoods full of light during the dark of winter awakens my spirit and makes me feel like celebrating.

Tonight, have a light celebration. Take a walk around your neighborhood with a friend, or suggest that your family hop in the car and scout out beautiful light displays together. Create a new family tradition of going out for an hour every night to look at lights in a different area. Drink hot chocolate and sing holiday music as you get into the holiday spirit by admiring the lights and decorations that others have put up for you to enjoy.

Off and On Friendships

Emily was my neighbor and I had known her since second grade. Even though we had been friends for a long time, she always ignored me at school. We hung out often after school and on the weekends, but I felt like she only wanted to be with me on her terms, like when there was nobody else around or if she had nothing better to do. I felt like she was embarrassed to be seen with me; when I saw her at school, she would walk by without even saying hello.

Friendships that are off and on are the worst kind to have. Don't put up with friends who use you or only talk to you in certain environments. A real friend will never act embarrassed to be around you. Although it is true that you will have many different friends in your life and only a few will become your best friends, all friends should always make time to say hi.

Private Self or Public Self?

I think that I have two very distinct personalities: private Amanda and public Amanda. My private side is thoughtful and passionate and keeps all my secret dreams, my views on the world, and my worst fears to myself. My public self is what I show to everyone around me; it is the censored version of my private self. I reveal only what I feel comfortable sharing and what I think other people will comfortable accepting.

Today, let yourself be vulnerable by sharing a bit of your inner self with people around you. Tell people some of your hopes for the future or reveal one of your biggest fears. We all have our public selves and private selves; however, the goal is to have our inner and outer be one and the same. When this happens, you are truly being yourself all the time.

No Need to Feel Guilty...

Has someone ever tried to make you feel guilty about something? Maybe your mother says, "You never spend time with the family," every time you ask if you can go out with your friends. Or maybe your friend says things like, "It's not fair that everything always works out for you." These people are using guilt to get you to do what they want.

Guilt trips are a sneaky tactic people use to get their way. Don't allow people to make you feel guilty for something that isn't your fault. When someone lays a guilt trip on you, just ignore it and do what you know in your heart is the right thing. If you know you haven't done anything wrong, you have no reason to feel guilty.

. . .Unless There's a Reason

You shouldn't feel guilty when you haven't done anything wrong, but there are legitimate reasons for feeling guilty. When you do something like cheat on a test, shoplift, or hurt somebody's feelings, you *should* listen to the feelings of guilt inside of you.

A guilty conscience is a sign that you have done something wrong, and it is up to you to fix the situation you're feeling remorseful about. Clear your guilty conscience by doing the right thing. Admit that you cheated on the test, return the item that you stole, or apologize to the person whose feelings you hurt. Although you may have to pay a penalty, doing the right thing will relieve the guilt that may otherwise stay with you for years.

Let guilt be your teacher—learn from the situation by thinking about how you would handle things differently next time to avoid feeling guilty.

Bah, Humbug!

Humbug to holiday spirit, to seasonal cheer, to peace on earth, and to a giving heart. That's right, humbug to buying gifts, to lighting candles, to decorating the house, to holiday cookies, and to being jolly. 'Tis the season to say, "Bah, Humbug!"

Are you feeling down in the dumps, tired, stressed, and anything but cheery? Maybe it's because you haven't gotten your humbugs out. This is holiday overload time and wherever you go, you see wreaths and carolers, which only leads you to conclude that even too much joy can be a terrible thing.

You're in luck because today is National Humbug Day. Write a list of twelve things you hate most about the holidays. Be Scrooge for a day and get your humbugs out so you don't have to carry them with you through the rest of the holidays and into the new year.

Be a Secretive Little Elf

Now that you've gotten your humbugs out, it's time to bring back the holiday cheer. One of the things that makes the holidays so special is the sense of magic that's in the air.

Today is your day to take part in that magic. Be a little elf and do anonymous acts that promote holiday cheer. Bake cookies and leave a plate of them on your teacher's desk, shovel snow off your neighbor's driveway, or make a holiday wreath and put it on your friend's locker. I once delivered a gift to a friend's house with a note that read, "Love, Santa." To this day, she still doesn't know who did it.

When you give without recognition, you create a feeling of magic that makes the holidays exciting for all.

Have a Night of Caroling

Music is one of the many wonderful things about the holidays. You can't help but feel jolly when you hear verses like "Dashing through the snow, in a one-horse open sleigh, over the fields we go, laughing all the way." Today, help to create some holiday joy by going caroling.

Gather your family, your friends, and your friends' families together for an evening of song. Type up the lyrics to some favorite holiday tunes, and hand out copies so that everyone knows the words. Remember to keep warm with gloves, scarves, blankets, and hot cider. Your group of carolers is bound to have a good time, and even if your voices aren't in perfect harmony, all who hear your holiday songs are bound to smile.

Sweet Anticipation

No anticipation is greater than a child's on Christmas Eve. After putting out a plate of cookies with a big glass of milk, I would lie in bed listening very carefully for Santa and his reindeer to visit my house. I was always the first one up on Christmas morning, and would spring out of bed before sunrise and wake my mother by yelling, "Santa came!" After I discovered that the presents under the tree were delivered by my mom instead of Santa, Christmas Eve no longer filled me with anticipation. During my teens, my mom often came into my room singing Christmas songs in order to get me up before noon.

What do you love most about Christmas Day? Is it the breakfast your mother cooks on Christmas morning, exchanging gifts with your family, or the sing-along your family has every year after dinner? Or, if you don't celebrate Christmas, think about what this time of year means to you and what you look forward to during this season. The feeling of anticipation is wonderful; get as excited as a child!

The Spirit of Christmas

Charles Dickens once wrote, "Oh would that Christmas lasted the whole year through as it ought. Would that the spirit of Christmas could live within our hearts every day of the year." What exactly is the "Christmas Spirit"? We know it's not about getting presents or having a vacation from school, although these things are often what we first associate with Christmas.

Tiny Tim, the crippled boy in Dickens' novel *A Christmas Carol,* is the personification of the Christmas Spirit. The youngest of his virtually penniless family, he never complains that he's ill and can't walk without a cane or that his Christmas dinner is small. He is the one who cheerfully proclaims, "God bless us, every one!"

Today, celebrate your wonderful life, give blessings to those you love, and wish for peace on earth. Today, live the Christmas Spirit!

I'm a Dreamer

My senior year of high school, I told a friend I wanted to write books. I shared my dream of writing stories about my life and being a published author. Laughing at me, she said, "Good luck! Your life had better get a lot more exciting if you want to write books. I doubt you'll ever be a published author."

I already have *two* books published! I didn't let my friend's negative remarks discourage me from pursuing my dream.

People always have negative things to say. Instead of encouraging us, friends tell us we won't succeed, teachers make us feel like we aren't smart enough, and parents say that our goals are unrealistic. It's time to stop paying attention to their pessimistic attitudes and tune into our deepest dreams and desires.

Dream big. You can do anything you set your mind to. Many people have done amazing things in spite of the discouraging comments they received. If the Wright brothers had listened to others, we wouldn't have airplanes today. Use the unsupportive thoughts to drive you forward. When you reach your goals, you will be able to look back and say, "I knew my dreams would come true!"

Taking Care of Your Toes

It can be very easy to forget about your feet during the winter. We hide them away in thick wool socks and stuff them into boots, or try to keep them warm in a pair of fuzzy slippers. Your poor feet probably haven't seen fresh air since August and could use a little revival.

Today, give yourself a wonderful winter pedicure. Fill your bathtub or a dishpan with warm water and let your feet soak. Scrub them with a washcloth and soap, smooth them with a pumice stone, rinse them with warm water, and pat them dry with a clean towel. Massage your feet with lotion, and then cut, file, and paint your toenails. When you are finished, slip your feet into a pair of comfy, warm slippers.

Just because your feet are out of sight during the winter months doesn't mean they don't deserve a bit of pampering.

Who Can Turn the World on with Her Smile?

When I couldn't sleep, I often flipped through infomercials and late night movies looking for something lighthearted to keep me company. One night, I miraculously stumbled across *The Mary Tyler Moore Show* and immediately fell in love with it. Hanging out with Mary Richards quickly became an addition to my nightly schedule, and my friends often made fun of my love for this far-from-trendy TV show they had never heard of before.

The opening song was one of the things I liked most about the show. With its catchy tune and uplifting lyrics, it always brought a smile to my face. Singing it gave me an instant confidence boost.

When you are feeling down or like the world has thrown you off course, singing or saying the words of this song can get you back on track. Today, search your *TV Guide* for *The Mary Tyler Moore Show*. The opening song is worth hearing!

See the Big Picture

As a teenager, it was often hard for me to look outside of my immediate world. I made decisions impulsively, based on how I felt at that moment, because I couldn't imagine life any differently from how it was in junior high and high school. As soon as I reached college, my teen years seemed like a distant memory.

Today, look at the big picture of your life. Think about how the decisions you are making at this time in your life will affect you ten years from now. Maybe all of your friends smoke, so it doesn't seem like a big deal to you right now. When you are twenty-five and trying to quit smoking, you will be kicking yourself for starting in the first place. The younger you are when you start doing things that aren't healthy for you, the harder it will be for you to change your bad habits. Today, ask yourself, "How will these decisions affect me when I'm older?" Stepping outside of your immediate situation and looking at the big picture is a sign of maturity.

What a Year It Has Been

With the calendar year coming to an end, now is a perfect time to sit and reflect on the past year. What has happened to you this year? How did you bring in the last New Year? What was summer like? Did the current school year get off to a good start?

Write a year-end summary in your journal. Title it "Oh, What a Year It Has Been," and write about what the past year has meant to you. Think about what you have learned over the past year. What mistakes did you make, and what experiences did you have that led you to discover something about yourself? What challenges did you face, and what have you learned from them? Who are your new friends this year? What events are you thankful for, and what could you have done without? What do you wish would have happened differently? What is your favorite thing that happened this year? How has this year helped you to become the person that you are today?

A List of Wishes
for the Year to Come

I never make New Year's resolutions because I never keep them. Resolutions are shallow, incomplete, and only focus on one specific part of your life.

Instead, I like to make a wish list for the year to come. Create a list that includes six categories: wishes for your mind—maybe you want to read at least five pleasure books; wishes for your body—you want to eat healthy or try out for the track team; wishes for your emotional life—you want to mourn the death of a loved one or forgive someone who has hurt you; wishes for your spirit—you want to feel closer to God or spend one day a week quietly listening to your soul; wishes for your actions—you want to smile at everyone you pass; and wishes for material life—you want a beautiful new dress.

There are no limitations on what you can wish for, so dig deep inside yourself and be specific. Keep this list someplace where you can look at it throughout the new year. Always remember that you have the power to make many of these wishes come true. Happy New Year!

Acknowledgments

What an amazing journey! Working on this book has taught me a great deal about writing and hard work as well as many things about my own mind and soul. Without the guidance, encouragement, love, and prayers of all who care about me and this project, I would never have had this growing experience.

I am incredibly grateful for my brilliant editor, Mary Jane Ryan. You believed in me and gave me the chance to make my vision a reality. Thank you for teaching me and for your intelligence and hard work. You always allowed me to voice my opinion and listened to my visions and hopes for the book.

My heartfelt appreciation to Ame Beanland for her artistic ideas and abilities and for covers extraordinaire!

Many thanks to everyone at Conari Press. I have learned that publishing a book takes a tremendous amount of creative energy, time, and dedication from an entire group of people—thank you allowing me to collaborate with you all. This book is as much yours as it is mine.

To Zach, for always listening and offering words of encouragement. You have been with me every step of the way—thank you.

Thank you to my wonderful friend Lindy, for your prayers and for always having only good things to say about me!

Last, but not least, to my roommate Aimee. Thank you for always listening to my brainstorms and for helping me come up with new ideas.

Resource Guide

Books and Web sites to be your companions as you grow, learn, fail, succeed, love, cry, smile, and laugh.

Books

33 Things Every Girl Should Know: Stories, Songs, Poems and Smart Talk by 33 Extraordinary Women. Tonya Bolden, ed. Crown Publications, 1998.
This collection offers thoughts, ideas, insights, and advice from well-known athletes, artists, writers, and entrepreneurs. Here you can see how successful women from many different backgrounds deal with different issues while growing up.

The Choice Is Yours: A Teenager's Guide to Self-Discovery, Relationships, Values, and Spiritual Growth. Bonnie M. Parsley. Fireside Books, 1992.
An encouraging book that helps teens develop qualities that are often difficult to acquire. Topics include self-love, learning self-discipline, relating to parents, and spiritual awareness.

Don't Give It Away, Iyanla Vanzant. Fireside Books, 1999.
A workbook in which you can write down your feelings and thoughts. This isn't just a journal; it's also filled

with information and thought-provoking questions and exercises.

Girl Power: Young Women Speak Out. Hillary Carlip. Warner Books, 1995.
Girls from ages thirteen to nineteen share their worries, hopes, dreams, and experiences. This book is full of stories, poems, letters, and notes from girls from all walks of life—cowgirls, teen mothers, lesbians, sorority girls, jocks, and gang girls.

Girltalk: All the Stuff Your Sister Never Told You. Carol Weston. HarperPerennial, 1997.
This book is full of all those things that you want to know but are too embarrassed to ask about, from personal hygiene to romance to anatomy to friendships.

The Holy Man. Susan Trott. Berkley Publishing Group, 1996.
Joyful and uplifting stories of a fictitious Holy Man and the people who want to meet him. This book teaches many lessons about life, values, spirituality, and self-discovery.

How to Survive the Loss of a Love. Harold H. Bloomfield, Melba Colgrove, and Peter McWillams. Prelude Press, 1993.
This book is helpful for dealing with any kind of loss you have suffered, whether the death of a family mem-

ber, a break-up, or the loss of a pet. This book helps to explain the feelings that accompany loss and gives advice for how to recover.

Real Girl, Real World: Tools for Finding Your True Self. Heath M. Gray, and Samantha Phillips. Seal Press, 1998.
Gives the facts on a wide range of topics from cosmetics to diets, to eating disorders to date rape to feminism. A frank and encouraging resource for girls.

The Seven Habits of Highly Effective Teens: The Ultimate Teenage Success Guide. Sean Covey. Simon and Schuster, 1998.
Step-by-step guides for improving self-image, creating values, achieving goals, communicating with family and friends, and more. Also, personal stories from teens around the world.

Sheroes. Varla Ventura. Conari Press, 1998.
Gives the profiles of hundreds of real and fictional heroines. A great place to find female role models.

Stay True: Short Stories for Strong Girls. Marilyn Singer, ed. Scholastic Paperbacks, 1999.
Fictional short stories by woman authors that depict teenage girls finding their inner strengths and overcoming struggles.

Web Sites

www.girlzone.com

Information and links to everything from fashion to travel to learning about ways to manage money. There are also contests in which girls can show off their diverse talents to win money and other prizes.

www.teenvoices.com

You can find poetry, stories, advice, volunteer and leadership opportunities, and a place to chat with other teens about issues that affect you all on this site. Also, check out their magazine, the first national publication written by and for teen women (1–888–882–TEEN).

www.go-girl.com

Learn the latest about fitness, school, fashion, and activities.

Index

To Our Readers

CONARI PRESS publishes books on topics ranging from spirituality, personal growth, and relationships to women's issues, parenting, and social issues. Our mission is to publish quality books that will make a difference in people's lives—how we feel about ourselves and how we relate to one another. We value integrity, compassion, and receptivity, both in the books we publish and in the way we do business.

As a member of the community, we sponsor the Random Acts of Kindness™ Foundation, the guiding force behind Random Acts of Kindness™ Week. We donate our damaged books to nonprofit organizations, dedicate a portion of our proceeds from certain books to charitable causes, and continually look for new ways to use natural resources as wisely as possible.

Our readers are our most important resource, and we value your input, suggestions, and ideas about what you would like to see published. Please feel free to contact us, to request our latest book catalog, or to be added to our mailing list.

2550 Ninth Street, Suite 101
Berkeley, California 94710-2551
800-685-9595 • 510-649-7175
fax: 510-649-7190 • e-mail: conari@conari.com
www.conari.com